Localising Chinese Language Curriculum Construction for Australian Primary School Students: Translanguaging Lens

超语视角下澳大利亚小学中文课程的本土化构建

赵昆鹏◎著

by Zhao Kunpeng

ZHEJIANG UNIVERSITY PRESS
浙江大学出版社
· 杭州 ·

CONTENTS

CHAPTER 1

Introduction

'zhōngwénrè – 中文热' (Chinese fever) is 'a term commonly used in the media to describe the increasing interest in learning Chinese that has coincided with China's growth as a global economic power' (Scrimgeour, 2014, p.151). For instance, according to the statistics provided by the National Asian Languages and Studies in Schools Program (NALSSP), the interest in learning Chinese in Australian schools has been growing (Sturak & Naughten, 2010). According to another group of notable figures, 92,931 students in Australia were studying Chinese in local schools in 2008 (Sturak & Naughten, 2010). Particularly, in New South Wales (NSW) the number of secondary school students who participated in the programs offered by the local Department of Education regarding Chinese language learning nearly arrived at over 20,000 in 2008, reflecting an increasing trend (Sturak &Naughten, 2010).

Conversely, the fact is that Australian school students' learning achievements in the Chinese language all over the nation are far less than they or the Australian government might have expected. As reported, more and more of the local young learners tend not to choose Chinese as their second language once they come to Year 11 or Year 12, as that language (Chinese) is no longer a compulsory course for them (Orton, 2008). They have many more alternative languages they can attempt to master, such as Japanese, French, or Korean. More importantly, such a plethora of choices contributes to the high dropout rate for the Chinese language programs, amounting to 94% among these local pupils (Orton, 2008).

By 2016, when it came to taking Chinese as a second language for Australian local school students, the dropout rate had steadily increased to 95% (Orton, 2016). Meanwhile, in terms of the Year 12 students, the beginning learners who preferred to continue engaging in learning the Chinese language had actually shrunk by 20% during the preceding 8 years (Orton, 2016). It is further concerning that Australian educational organisations are confronted with the reality that it is difficult to cultivate and provide bilingual expertise (between English and Chinese) which is urgently needed by the local labour market (Orton, 2016). Considering that, the learning of the Chinese language by predominantly monolingual English-speaking learners in Australia is 'as fragile as fine bone china' (Singh & Ballantyne, 2014, p.200) for whom English is their 'everyday language of instruction and communication' (Singh & Han, 2014, p.410). That is to say, it is a challenge to facilitate Chinese language learning among non-native beginning learners in English-speaking school communities.

It is worth mentioning that the Australian Curriculum, Assessment and Reporting Authority (ACARA) speaks of the 'Background Language Learners' (2013, p.4), and thus by this implication suggests that other learners would be called 'Non-Background Language Learners.' However, ACARA refers to them as 'Second Language Learners' instead. For ACARA, 'Second Language Learners' refers to students learning Chinese as a second or additional language. Thus, to avoid classifying students in a deficit way, terms such as 'non-background,' 'non-native,' and 'monolingual speakers' have not been used in this study. Here, 'Emergent Second Language Learners' is used in this study to refer to the primary school students for whom English is their everyday, recurring language of instruction and communication who were in Stage 2 and Stage 3, with limited knowledge of Chinese.

1.1 The ROSETE Program

The particular case engaged in this study is entitled Research Oriented, School Engaged Teacher-Researcher Education (ROSETE) Program. As the name suggests, ROSETE is an education program which is targeted at cultivating and supplying capable, suitable Chinese teachers for Australian school students through examining and solving pedagogical issues and cultural barriers in making Chinese learnable for the local learners, especially for those who primarily use English for their daily learning (Singh & Han, 2014). Such a program was initiated by a partnership among three parties, including the New South Wales Department of Education and Communities (Australia), the Ningbo Municipal Education Bureau (China) and the Western Sydney University, since 2008 (Singh & Han, 2014). That partnership has shaped the development of the ROSETE Program, in particular for the facilitation of Chinese teacher-researchers' education (Han & Yao, 2013; Singh & Ballantyne, 2014). Being in such a partnered status between Australia and China, this program is dedicated to equipping Chinese teacher-researchers with the expertise to develop their future career trajectories in both local and international educational industries (Singh & Han, 2014).

Characteristically, the ROSETE Program integrates the education of the teacher-researchers into their daily teaching practices as Chinese volunteer teachers in the local primary and secondary schools of NSW (Singh & Han, 2014). More importantly, the teacher-researchers are necessarily engaged in workshops, lectures, and sessions on utilising such evidence-driven methodologies to make Chinese learnable for Australian local school students (Singh & Han, 2014). By doing so, these teacher-researchers are able not only to grow into qualified teachers of Chinese as a local/global language, but also to accumulate their research abilities by generating the knowledge both driven by the empirical evidence in practice, and informed by the theoretical concepts, thus ultimately increasing the learnability of Chinese for the Australian primary and secondary school pupils in such English-monolingual educational settings.

Being engaged in a research-oriented, school-engaged educational program for teaching Chinese, the terminology 'teacher-researcher' is employed in this research project, which means undertaking dual roles. On the one hand, the conductor of this study acts as a Chinese teacher in class, delivering lessons to the Stage 2 and Stage 3 students in alocal primary school in NSW. On the other hand, working as a researcher involves collecting and analysing the relevant evidence from daily Chinese teaching practices, as well as assuming the responsibility for reporting the corresponding research findings in the form of a degree thesis and making original contributions to the academic research community.

1.2 Research Problems

The ROSETE Program is committed to making Chinese learnable for Australian school students in the local educational environment. It aims to effectively integrate Chinese language education into its research-oriented teaching process (Singh & Han, 2015). The core mechanism of such a program lies in forming a 'chain,' combining the practical teaching action (school-engaged) with the original knowledge production (research-oriented) in the field of Chinese language education (Singh & Han, 2015). The various factors behind the high dropout rate among the beginning learners of Chinese in the Australian educational milieu were explored. Initially, determining what to teach to these beginning learners becomes the central issue, as existing Chinese learning materials, including textbooks and curriculum requirements are lacking in locally cultural and educational appropriateness (Zhao & Huang, 2010). It also entails that native Chinese speakers who teach Chinese should be capable of departing from the local beginning learners' (the Australian school students) characteristics to capture their real needs and perceptions regarding learning Chinese in the local context, thus making Chinese a local and learnable language for them (Singh & Han, 2014; Singh & Han, 2015). In this sense, developing instructive resources which are culturally appropriate and high in content-learnability for those beginning learners is considered as an essential way to achieve this goal.

Another major concern for the current situation of Chinese language teaching is 'the alienation of beginning learners' due to the employment of such a 'monolingual theoretic-pedagogical framework' as the set of instruction strategies (Singh & Han, 2015, p.168). It is thus emphasised that such modes of teaching Chinese are aimed at beginning learners in China (Tsung & Cruickshank, 2010). Consequently, the adoption of de-contextualised and teacher-directed instruction approaches to teaching beginning learners makes them feel that learning Chinese is very demanding and less rewarding (Zhang & Li, 2010). This means that the learning materials adopted and the courses designed for the overseas Chinese learners are inclined to be constructed and developed from the perspective of the language itself and native Chinese teachers, without taking the overseas students' interests and features into consideration (Zhang & Li, 2010).

It is worth mentioning that the teacher-researcher has experienced a similar situation before conducting this study. At that time, the teacher-researcher was allocated to a local secondary school in NSW, Australia, for the preparation and observation of his independent Chinese language teaching. Consequently, the teacher-researcher not only gained a sound understanding concerning the local school students' preferences in terms of what they desire to learn from Chinese class, but can also identify their innate characteristics regarding how they can be engaged in mastering Chinese in their familiarised learning styles. In light of such preparatory work, the teacher-researcher's inherent beliefs have been modified, and this may influence the acclimatising of his Chinese teaching practices to the schoolchildren's learning aptitudes and habits in the Australian educational system (Moloney & Xu, 2015b).

Apart from the above-mentioned issues encountered in teaching Chinese to beginning learners in the global context, other challenges concerning Chinese teaching in Australian schools were identified as 'the extremely limited attention to pedagogy, resources, teacher professional development and training for Chinese in primary schools' (Moloney & Xu, 2018, p.20). Also, it is claimed that 'the limited exposure time and the week gap between lessons' undoubtedly require more diverse and creative teaching methods to strengthen pupils' learning achievements and maintain their interest in those school Chinese programs (Moloney & Xu, 2018).

The teacher-researcher encountered such a situation as the students in this case study school had just one Chinese lesson of roughly 40 minutes for Stage 2 and Stage

3 students each week. That is to say, fewer opportunities were provided for these children to be exposed to using Chinese in the local educational environment. Also, there was a huge gap between weekly Chinese lessons. For example, sometimes the students would be involved in other school activities, including swimming and chess competitions, signing and dancing practice, or performance rehearsals. All these problems confronted by the teacher-researcher in his daily teaching experiences unavoidably put some burdens on making Chinese learnable for the local school students.

Afterwards, when the teacher-researcher followed the Australian K-10 Chinese syllabus for designing the daily Chinese lesson plans, some questions and confusions still arose. In terms of their anticipated spoken ability, local students were often expected to learn how to engage in conversations using sentence patterns such as, 'Qǐng wèn – 请问 ……?(May I ask ... ?)' (BOSTES, 2003, p.30). This is a representative verbal expression which can occur in a dialogue between teacher and student to very politely make a request in China. In fact, such a linguistic term is no longer popular or applicable in real classrooms in China, as it has been outmoded and is impractical for emergent second-language learners of Chinese. At the same time, cultivating the local school students' communicative abilities is regarded as the core goal, while operating within the bounds of the Chinese language as a system (BOSTES, 2003). Considering that, it is likely that the teacher-researcher's attention may be transferred to the language itself, disregarding the students' perspectives. Not surprisingly, local school students gradually tend to quit learning Chinese, while preferably choosing other languages as their second language if necessary, thereby slowly diminishing any 'zhōngwénrè – 中文热' to some extent.

Therefore, the Chinese teacher-researcher is disposed to probe into the proper learning content sources and workable instruction strategies based on the fundamental guidelines in BOSTES (2003), AITSL (2012), and ACARA (2013) to construct a tailored Chinese curriculum that takes into account various Australian cultural considerations, and then generate the localised Chinese learning materials for Australian school students, eventually making contributions to further develop such educational documents. Naturally, the research focus of this study is self-elicited through such a research problem being addressed here.

1.3 Research Focus

Inspired by the aforementioned research problems, teaching Chinese after taking into consideration Australian school students' characteristics and preferences has been taken as the primary strategy for the sustainable learning of the Chinese language in the local educational environment (Zhu, 2010; Singh & Han, 2014). Specifically, the school-engaged research projects for producing the retention tactics will prioritise constructing a corpus of learning content by means of exploiting Australian pupils' recurring everyday sociolinguistic activities as performed in English in the school communities (Singh, Han & Ballantyne, 2014; Singh & Han, 2014; Singh & Han, 2015). What is more, being informed by the notion of 'language as a local practice' (Pennycook, 2010) provides the possibility of making Chinese the embodiment of various local practices. In this regard, local school students' interest in Chinese language tends to be maintained through being exposed to rewarding experiences in such contextualised learning spaces as those established in Chinese classes (Singh & Han, 2014; Harreveld & Singh, 2009). In terms of making Chinese learnable through 'localisation,' it is further put forward that 'language and and literacy are situated social practices' (Singh & Nguyễn, 2018, p.200), which is targeted at constructing 'a context which frames its uses and gives it a place where it can take hold in students' everyday lives' (Singh & Nguyễn, 2018, p.200).

At the same time, 'localising Chinese' entails that Chinese teachers 'are able to plan and implement lessons relating what the students already know in English to the Chinese they are to learn and use locally through getting to know their students' (Singh & Nguyễn, 2018, p.200). However, it is argued that native Chinese teachers prefer to base their teaching on the pedagogical doctrine of being teacher-directed, rather than student-centred, which can ignore the local students' knowledge base shaped by their former learning experiences in the school-based community. For that reason, it is difficult to engage local students with the learning content due to the existing ineffective teaching approaches (Duff et al., 2013; Singh & Han, 2014). However, the concept of 'funds of knowledge' (González, Moll & Amanti, 2005) tends to equip the teacher-researcher with an alternative perspective to activate and involve the local students' intellectual resources accumulated in the monolingual

(English-speaking) educational context for enhancing their learning of Chinese.

The above-mentioned phenomenon provide the teacher-researcher with some practical directions and methods regarding how to localise Chinese, namely taking the teacher-researcher out of a concept of teaching Chinese as an 'alien language,' or 'an abstract linguistic system that is a decontextualised entity operating outside the students' everyday lives' (Singh & Nguyễn, 2018, p.200). Therefore, to embody such notions and judge their effectiveness in making Chinese learnable in the real teaching and learning context, the research focus of this study is to explore local school students' daily recurring sociolinguistic activities (what to teach) and mobilise their funds of knowledge (how to teach) which have accumulated in the school-based community. This school-based community can be utilised as the learning content sources and instruction strategies for constructing a localised and student-centred Chinese curriculum, to enrich their learning of Chinese in the Australian educational milieu. To do so, the teacher-researcher initially gathers examples of forms of the local students' recurrent sociolinguistic activities that they perform in English in the school-based community. After that, these linguistic repertoires collected are utilised as the learning content sources for the Chinese curriculum construction, by drawing on examples from their daily speech practices at school. In the meanwhile, employing appropriate teaching methods is indispensable in recognising and deploying the local students' knowledge configurations. Being guided by a student-centred pedagogy, the teacher-researcher adopts multidimensional instruction strategies for mobilising their funds of knowledge developed in the school-based community to reinforce their learning of such localised content.

Accordingly, this research project specifies the forms of Australian students' daily recurring sociolinguistic activities used for creating the localised Chinese learning content. It also extends students' funds of knowledge shaped in the school-based community to the field of Chinese language education for eliciting appropriate instruction strategies. Effectively integrating the above two essential elements into Chinese curriculum construction is beneficial for enacting local school students' potential translanguaging aptitudes, as their emergent bilingual identity is transferred between English and Chinese within the situated learning atmosphere (García, 2009; García & Kleifgen, 2010; Creese & Blackledge, 2010; Canagarajah, 2011;

Wei, 2011; Lave & Wenger, 1991). That is to say, this research project intends to address issues relating to translanguaging pedagogical approaches rather than the issues relating to the scope and sequence required for curriculum design in terms of creating a meaningful accumulated linguistic sequence. Meanwhile, it is worth mentioning that this study is based on the *Australian Professional Standards for Teachers* (2012) to select and develop content sources and pedagogical approaches for the purpose of developing not just a localised, but also a student-centred curriculum, ultimately conducting effective Chinese teaching and learning in an engaging environment. Nevertheless, the focus is not on sitting within a systematised sequence of language acquisition in relation to the scope required for curriculum design. By doing so, this study ultimately proposes a sociolinguistic activities-based and funds of knowledge-oriented approach to the localised and student-centred Chinese curriculum construction, and verifies its efficacy in terms of making Chinese learnable in the Australian educational milieu. In view of that, it is anticipated that its potential suitability and effectiveness will be mobilised and transferred to more emergent second language learners of Chinese worldwide, with a special emphasis on their unique localities.

To explain the above-mentioned situation, this study concentrates on local students' daily recurring sociolinguistic activities, along with their funds of knowledge in the school-based community, which enable them to become co-constructors of Chinese knowledge so that they can be equally dialogic in Chinese class, thereby empowering their agency and helping build their identity in learning Chinese. Such a research setting is to be envisioned based on the following research questions proposed within the boundary set for the present research project. Being informed by the research problem and focus as aforesaid, the major research question addressed in this study is as follows:

> How can the use of students'sociolinguistic activities and funds of knowledge contribute to curriculum construction to enrich the learning of the Chinese language?

To better direct the teacher-researcher to collect and interpret information throughout the research process, the following three inter-related contributory research questions are set out:

CR1: What forms of the local students'daily recurring sociolinguistic activities in the school-based community can the Chinese teacher-researcher utilise as content sources for curriculum construction? (What to Teach)

CR2: How can the Chinese teacher-researcher mobilise the local students' funds of knowledge shaped in the school-based community through the process of interacting with their learning of Chinese? (How to Teach)

These evolved research questions were employed to guide the production of evidence, and were elaborated upon during the process of conducting this study and responded to in the evidentiary chapter 8 and chapter 9 respectively. Through searching for the answers to these research questions, this research project looks into alternative and effective ways to construct a workable and suitable Chinese curriculum facilitated by utilising the students' daily recurring sociolinguistic activities and mobilising their funds of knowledge accumulated in the school-based community. This creates the opportunity for developing localised and student-centred curricula, aimed at making Chinese learnable. To answer the research questions, the proper research approach is proposed in the following section.

1.4 Case Study as the Research Approach

Case study as a traditional method in qualitative research is predominantly selected for its power in facilitating thorough examinations of social phenomena in their tangible situations, despite encountering a few contestations in terms of its rigour and transferability. Moreover, it is an effective research tactic that can focus rigorous attention on a handful of participants and allow issues to be explored profoundly (Yin, 2018; Robson & McCartan, 2016; Swanborn, 2010; Cohen, Manion & Morrison, 2011). That is to say, case studies tend to be carried out to recognise real-life issues, especially when 'phenomenon and context are not always sharply distinguishable in real-world situations' (Yin, 2018, p.15). Similarly, Cohen et al. (2011) state that a case study 'provides a unique example of real people in real situations, enabling readers to understand ideas more clearly than simply by presenting them with abstract theories or principles' (p.289).

This research project focuses on curriculum construction for Chinese language learning by exploring students' daily recurring sociolinguistic activities and funds of knowledge within the context of an Australian local school. It aims to investigate how the Chinese teacher-researcher can utilise these local resources for constructing a localised and student-centered curriculum of Chinese language learning, and how this can contribute to the development of Chinese language education practices. Given the above-mentioned characteristics and benefits, as well as the proposed research problem and focus, a case study is preferred and adopted as the research method for this study.

Specifically, the study explored what can be done to make (spoken) Chinese learnable for Australian local school students through engaging in an Australia-China partnership program entitled the ROSETE Program. It starts with looking into the students' daily activities, as performed in English, as well as the categories of their knowledge base shaped in a local public school in NSW. The value of such a departure point lies in two major respects. On the one hand, it is to discover learnable content sources in the local educational milieu. On the other hand, it is targeted at implementing teachable strategies based on the local students' accustomed learning habits. In this regard, this study has a tendency towards collecting the local students' linguistic and cultural repertoires accumulated in their English-speaking school-based community, for theorising the localised and student-centred Chinese curriculum construction. Furthermore, it is anticipated that the mobility and learnability of the Chinese language for these emergent second language learners will be improved, thus reducing the growing dropout rate observed among these Chinese learning programs.

1.4.1 Site Selection

A physical 'place' is a necessity for a 'case' such as this one which happens in the real world. A case study can be a 'one case (single) study' or a 'several cases (multiple) study' (Swanborn, 2010, p.21). In this research project, a local public school was selected and constructed as the research 'place' or site for this single-case study, which is a welcoming and innovative school located in the Western Sydney Region (WSR) of NSW. More importantly, it is one of the partner schools of the ROSETE Program where the teacher-researcher was engaged in performing his daily Chinese teaching and undertaking the current research project during a certain period of time (between 30/06/2016 and 20/12/2017). Meanwhile, a pseudo-Chinese name – 剑桥花园小学 (Jiànqiáo Huāyuán Xiǎoxué) was given to protect the privacy of the relevant participants and stakeholders from this school.

As its name suggests, this local public school does take great pride in providing a safe and purposeful learning environment leading to the development of successful citizens. The school is well known for its academic focus, extensive opportunities in extracurricular activities and strong community involvement. It continues to increase the use of technology across all key learning areas. The core value of this selected public school is to focus on innovative programs and practices, to deliver excellence in student achievement, as well as to connect with parents, community and the wider world. All the above-mentioned are also regarded as positive factors that deeply influenced the planned investigation and the teacher-researcher's Chinese teaching practices.

This public school had no Chinese language courses until they were generated by the native Chinese volunteer teachers from the ROSETE Program who came to this school, working as the Chinese teacher-researchers for the local children. At the same time, the principal, classroom teachers, and other staff at this school showed full willingness to participate in this educational and research program and to provide necessary support throughout the teaching and research process. It is worth mentioning here that there existed various challenges and difficulties in conducting multiple sites of fieldwork due to time and financial limits, and particularly the ethical considerations. Therefore, a single-sited case study is a reasonable choice for this school-based research, not only because of limited time and funding resources, but also because of its peaceful and respectful learning environment for teaching and research.

1.4.2 Participant Recruitment

The researcher in this study was a Chinese volunteer teacher from the ROSETE

Program. To be exact, while teaching Chinese at this local public school the teacher-researcher was undertaking his research project as well through participating in such a school-based and research-oriented program. The students from Stage 2 (Year 3 & Year 4) and Stage 3 (Year 5) were allocated to the teacher-researcher. This participant group shared the following relevant characteristics. At the very beginning, these participants were all students with age range from 8 to 12 in the researcher's Chinese class at the school where he volunteered in Chinese language teaching. Additionally, they were English speakers. However, most of them had some/limited Chinese language exposure in kindergarten and Stage 1, and a small proportion of them had diverse linguistic backgrounds. The project aimed to explore how the local students' everyday recurring sociolinguistic activities and their funds of knowledge in the school-based community can be employed to enrich their learning of Chinese as a foreign language. The characteristics of this participant group which were relevant to the aims of the project are as follows:

1. The participants were students in a Western Sydney school.
2. The participants were Year 3, Year 4, and Year 5 students who chose to learn Chinese in the teacher-researcher's class.
3. All of them were English-monolingual learners and non-native speakers of Chinese and most of them only had a few prior experiences of Chinese language in their earlier schooling. The participants were beginning learners of Chinese.

Another participant group was the five classroom teachers in this local public school. They were local school students' classroom teachers who assisted in managing the class when the teacher-researcher was giving the Chinese lessons, as he lacked the requisite Australian Teacher Qualification Certificate to teach on his own. Within this capacity, this group of participants helped the teacher-researcher observe the students' classroom performance and engagement. They also gave constructive comments and effective feedback on the Chinese lessons delivered after integrating the students' everyday recurring sociolinguistic activities, frequently used language, as well as their preferred instruction styles regarding Chinese language learning. For such multifaceted reasons and considerations, these were the participants chosen to be in this study.

These three types of participants formed three sorts of data sources and essentially constructed the triangulation for the research project. It enabled the teacher-researcher to collect overall data from manifold angles, offering multiple involvements and perceptions. Figure 1.1 displays an overall information concerning the actual selection process and constituents of the research site and participants.

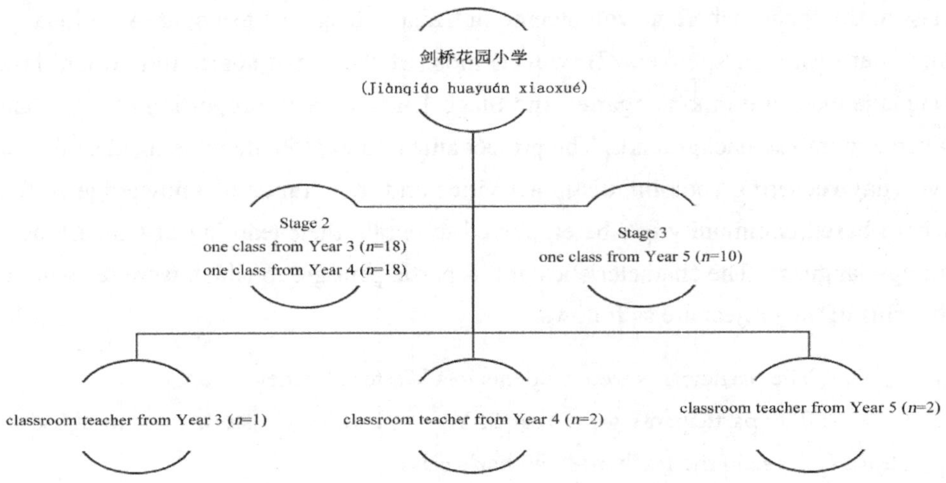

Figure 1.1 An Overview of the Research Site and Participants

1.4.3 Data Collection

Three methods of data collection were employed in this case study, including the unstructured observations, photo-elicitation interviews, and the collection of relevant documents. Two categories of data were produced and collected, namely the transcripts from the interviews and the texts from the observations and documents. One research site (a public school in NSW) was adopted to collect this data. An overview for generating the data sources and types is displayed in Figure 1.2.

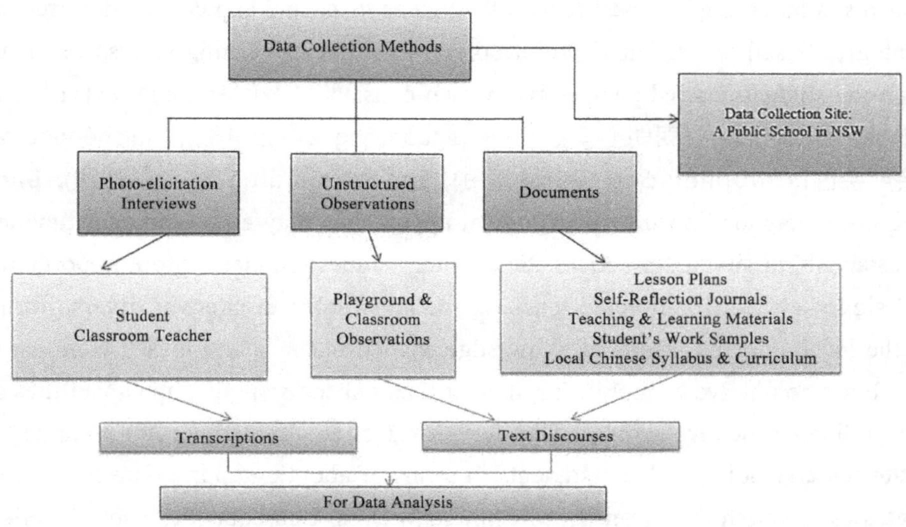

Figure 1.2 An Overview of Data Sources and Types

In the next section, the structure of argument explains how this book is constructed and developed.

1.5 Structure of Argument

This book suggests a students' sociolinguistic activities-based and funds of knowledge-oriented approach of constructing a localised and student-centred curriculum for enhancing the learning of Chinese in the Australian educational setting. Firstly, it discovers the Australian students' daily recurring sociolinguistic activities undertaken in English in a local primary school. Meanwhile, being aware of these everyday happenings in school helps the teacher-researcher to capture and generate the localised and learnable content sources through the students' mutual negotiations and decision-making in Chinese class. Following that, this book puts forward three alternative perspectives, from the indigenous Chinese metaphors 'liàngtǐcáiyī' (量体裁衣), 'jiùdìqǔcái' (就地取材) and 'zhǔrénwēng yìshí' (主人翁意识), to better appreciate the local students' preferences towards the learning content.

In this book, it discusses the teacher-researcher's endeavours in engaging local students in mastering localised content through devising and implementing instruction strategies based on students' preferred and habituated learning styles, departing from the student-centred perspective, which consists of 'xǐwénlèjiàn' (喜闻乐见), 'lǎnglǎngshàngkǒu' (朗朗上口), 'rónghuìguàntōng' (融会贯通), 'huìshēnghuìsè' (绘声绘色), 'wùjìnqíyòng' (物尽其用), and 'rénjìnqícái' (人尽其才). Such Chinese metaphor-informed pedagogical approaches play a predominant function of establishing situated practices for learning Chinese in class. More importantly, utilising such learner-directed teaching methods helps to uncover diverse forms of the local students' funds of knowledge shaped in the school-based community which are conducive to mobilising their influential translanguaging capabilities as their bilingual identity evolves. That further offers an alternative route to having a better understanding of local students in terms of adopting appropriate instruction strategies to enrich their learning of Chinese in class. Consequently, a set of student knowledge-oriented instruction strategies is nominated to deploy their knowledge base for constructing the student-centred Chinese curriculum. This pedagogical belief is bestowed with the possibility of enabling local school students' agency to decide on their favoured (but still appropriate) Chinese teaching strategies in such a way that they will be equally dialogic in class.

This book identifies the achieved Chinese learning outcomes after utilising such localised learning content and student-centred instruction strategies for Australian local school students in the actual Chinese classes. To further activate and transfer such suitability and learnability for more emergent Chinese language learners around the world, the principle of 'yīndìzhìyí' (因地制宜) needs to be given priority, after considering the differentiated cultural and educational factors.

CHAPTER 2

Curriculum Construction for Chinese Language Teaching and Learning

Having presented a general overview of the research problem concerning the current Chinese teaching and learning techniques, it is obvious that there is limited access to appropriate teaching and learning materials for Chinese language education (e.g. textbooks and curricula) that are designed from the perspectives of the diverse beginning Chinese learners of the world (Zhang & Li, 2010). Meanwhile, the scarcity of instruction approaches, focusing on the overseas Chinese learners' daily preferred learning styles in schools, also creates more barriers to making Chinese learnable for them (Orton, 2008; Zhang & Li, 2010). Therefore, this section reviews the literature concerning the multidimensional aspects that need to be addressed in terms of constructing suitable curricula for different learners in the process of mastering novel knowledge.

In a general sense, curriculum is defined as 'what is taught to learners,' which includes 'the intended and unintended information, skills, and attitudes that are communicated to learners whether in schools or in other locations where teaching takes place' (Sowell, 2005, p.4). Under this circumstance, the process of curriculum construction tends to be subject to the selection of various content sources, serving the multi-instructive objectives (Sowell, 2005). Accordingly, curriculum construction is a process that includes 'a series of decisions and judgements' which are based on the designer's 'beliefs, assumptions, perceptions, and biases' (Smith & Lovat, 2003, p.2). As for the curriculum developers, they need to use their knowledge and skills to 'make the best decisions, to choose the most appropriate or justifiable alternatives' when learners, teachers, resources, and learning contexts are taken into consideration (Smith & Lovat, 2003, p.25). Nonetheless, it is pointed out that it is impossible for educators to produce an inclusive curriculum for 'generic students' as such a process of curriculum construction is prone to conceiving of learners as 'receivers of knowledge' as opposed to 'sources of knowledge' (Sleeter & Carmona, 2016, p.100). Therefore, these and other corresponding concerns identified by the teacher-researcher are explored in the following subsections.

2.1 Concerns Occurring in the Process of Curriculum Construction

There is a concern as to how 'perfect decisions' can be made, and how proper and reasonable alternatives can be proposed during the whole process of curriculum construction. As the curriculum construction process is related to knowledge selection and representation, it is concerned with the reality of 'creating agency' that inevitably involves a curriculum developer's particular standpoint regarding the selection of content sources, teaching content, and learning tasks to a large extent (Smith & Lovat, 2003, p.34). Meanwhile, as indicated by the philosophy of 'curriculum as content,' curriculum construction is mainly viewed as a process of simply transmitting knowledge from teachers to students, with power centred at the instructors' knowledge bases and the importance of examining the learned information (Ord, 2016, p.35). Accordingly, such an approach is vividly defined as the 'banking model' that regards pupils as 'empty vessels into which knowledge is poured for retrieval later,' as the constructed curricula tend to alienate their localised learning environments (Sleeter & Carmona, 2016, p.101). Correspondingly, Sleeter and Carmona (2016) have compared the curriculum construction process to 'pottery making' (p.52), linking it to the 'big picture' around curriculum construction which not only strictly abides by the standardised national requirements, but also needs to blend into crafted knowledge with differentiated personalities as the 'pottery maker.'

That is to say, it inevitably involves the designer's intended perspectives and ends during the process of curriculum construction. Therefore, it is difficult for curriculum planners to balance multiple alternatives, given the ideal that decision-making should satisfy different curriculum consumers' needs and interests.

2.2 Repositioning Content Sources for Curriculum Construction

To echo such concerns which arise during the process of curriculum construction, the efforts involved in reshaping the content sources for the existing Australian curriculum, especially in learning the Chinese language, require that:

> A curriculum for Australia needs to begin with the recognition of the diverse linguistic, cultural, and personal life-worlds of students, that is, their intra-culturality; it needs to reflect the lived realities of these diverse students...The social and cultural life-worlds of students' reference not only their backgrounds, understood as the context for learning, but rather, their prior experiences that constitute learning. Students are unique social and cultural beings who interpret the world through their own social and cultural traditions, understandings, and values. Their learning depends on an education process that takes this into account (Scarino, 2010, p.168).

According to this statement, the multilayered forms of the learners' knowledge bases should be valued, triggered, and well-utilised as meaningful content sources to enable their learning to take place in a contextualised space (Sleeter & Carmona, 2016). They point out that curriculum resources are analogous to 'mirrors' (p.137) and 'windows' (p.143) through which students tend to positively attach the learning stuff to their existing knowledge from their real-life practices, thus improving their academic outcomes through engaging with such content (Sleeter & Carmona, 2016).

Also, to prevent the alternatives being chosen from relying heavily on the curriculum designers' knowledge and perceptions regarding the curriculum content, various perspectives (e.g. 'student-centred perspective') (p.16) need to be taken into account (Marsh, 2009). Smith and Lovat also highlight (2003) that 'knowledge and cultural experiences' (p.33) are valuable and effective curriculum content sources in contributing to mastering certain knowledge for learners in a specific context. As stated by Sowell (2005), 'curriculum content is the raw material for student learning in schools' (p.152). Meanwhile, given the criteria concerning the selection of sources for curriculum content, 'learnability by learners' (p.157) and 'appropriateness for needs-interests of learners' (p.158) are regarded as the two fundamental principles (Sowell, 2005). Learnability is closely connected to learners' abilities for whose knowledge is adopted as curriculum content sources, which shows how highly curricula designers value learners' previous and existing knowledge (Sowell, 2005). Another aspect which needs considering is the suitability of curriculum content for learners' enduring needs and interests (Sowell, 2005). It is suggested that curriculum developers should actively employ students' established knowledge for the screening of curriculum content sources during the process of their social, household, and school development (Sowell, 2005).

Furthermore, it is suggested that all the planned and intended decision-making concerning the choices of curriculum content need to be put into classroom teaching and learning practices in the school-based context (Smith & Lovat, 2003). Namely, students' existing knowledge is an indispensable component of the content sources in the process of curriculum construction as they are the 'ultimate consumers' (p.212) of curriculum (Marsh, 2009). For that reason, students are seen as potential resources for curriculum construction, especially when they are situated in a culture-related and learning-interest-based environment (Sleeter & Carmona, 2016). To strengthen the significance of knowledge sources, as well as to establish a contextualised curriculum, Li (2017) emphasises that:

> Letting our curriculum return to social practices as a community is an inexhaustible resource, which has an impact on us, guides students and supports children's lives there. Life scenarios seem to narrate their past lives and bring lots of deep thinking, meanwhile calling people to look into the future. Indeed, life itself is a textbook as well and the best experimental area for children's learning, the most vivid classroom of comprehensive practices. It makes no sense if the child's knowledge is far away from society or separate from life, when as a result

they cannot comprehend the essentials of knowledge (p.5).

The idea of drawing on students' real-life experiences within their community-related context would provide curriculum constructors and learners with resourceful teaching and learning materials and activities. To be exact, students' daily life experiences are profound educational resources that can be activated and exploited, and can be helpful in turning abstract knowledge into tangible everyday practices, achieving the ultimate purpose of better understanding and using learned knowledge in actual situations. Therefore, students can supply various and valuable perspectives and become practical contributors to curriculum construction and development in a circumstance whereby they are empowered as the 'optimum agency.'

2.3 Problems in the Australian Curriculum for Chinese Teaching and Learning

Given the importance of the criteria in selecting curriculum content sources, this section intends to investigate the learnability and the appropriateness of the Australian curriculum for local school students in learning the Chinese language based on the analysis of relevant literature.

The Australian Research Centre for Languages Education has been responsible for curriculum development in teaching Asian languages at both national and state levels for many decades. However, there are no distinctive criteria to gauge students' learning outcomes in mastering different Asian languages due to the generic, generalised and standardised construction of curricula (Scarino, 2014). As for the learning outcomes of one Asian language (e.g. Chinese), it has been outlined as the communicative purpose in the Australian local context. Nevertheless, such an objective has lost its essential power due to the decrease in the hands-on use of the target language in daily life (Scarino, 2014). Having examined the relevant Australian language documents aimed at widening Chinese language teaching for the local primary and secondary school students, the exigency is to construct an Australian children's 'exclusive,' while in some respects an 'inclusive,' curriculum for learning Chinese based on their various community-related social practices and

Australian particularities, thereby being helpful for the students in shaping a positive identity for them as they gain Chinese language knowledge (Möllering, 2015). Thus, it is vital to recognise the prominence of the local students' prior, existing and powerful knowledge from their school-based linguistic and cultural practices, as that sort of knowledge formed and maintained within such a community setting is of value in constructing a learnable Chinese language curriculum.

Admittedly, ACARA (2013 revised version for languages: Chinese) has made many improvements, in that different needs, perspectives, and backgrounds of various learner groups, including second language learners, background language learners and first language learners, are now recognised and delineated. Nonetheless, it is contended that the developed curriculum for learning Chinese should be built on the local students' sociolinguistic activities and lived experiences in the Australian milieu (Scrimgeour, 2014). Accordingly, the major criticism is focused on the struggle to discover appropriate Chinese learning resources for the reason that such authorised curriculum content for Chinese language teaching in Australian schools attaches little connection to the local students' cultural and daily practices (Chen & Zhang, 2014). In order to solve this problem, an antidote entitled 'corpus strategies' has been proposed to mediate the transfer from the learners' prior L1 sociolinguistic (English language) knowledge to the L2 (Chinese language) learning by involving the partial cross-sociolinguistic similarities between the two languages (Singh & Ballantyne, 2014; Singh & Han, 2015). Considering the aforementioned problems, it is not surprising to find out that the Australian language curriculum for Chinese language learning fails to deliberately recognise the local school students' valuable knowledge and effectively use this knowledge as the content source for curriculum construction (Ditchburn, 2012). Consequently, the peripheral students' engagement and interest in learning Chinese are likely to be hindered or impaired due to the one-size-fits-all national language curriculum. Furthermore, it is recommended that 'students' lives, perspectives, cultures and experiences' should be utilised as some of the several content sources of curriculum construction so that students can work as the 'co-constructors and co-creators (rather than passive consumers) of that curriculum' (Smyth, 2010, p.191). That is to say, according to the new national model and criteria on curriculum construction for learning Asian languages, the

'creativity and use of alternative learning resources' (p.42) should be encouraged to develop 'a learnable not teachable curriculum' (p.39) in attempting to fulfil the demands of the new generation of Chinese learners in the Australian context (Crawford, 2012).

The content of curriculum construction should be negotiated to enhance its flexibility and applicability for CFL (Chinese as a Foreign Language) curriculum internationalisation (Wang, Moloney & Li, 2013). The professional learning program designed for CFL teachers is required to take teachers' creativity and employability into consideration to make pedagogical knowledge content (PKC) widely accessible for CFL curriculum construction. As for CFL teacher-researchers in Australian schools, the influential factors on teachers' self-efficacy include the teachers' expertise in the medium of instruction, professional learning, teaching experience, and knowledge of students (Chen & Yeung, 2015). In the meantime, it is suggested that such impacts are beneficial for accelerating the development of resourceful curricular and innovative pedagogies for teaching Chinese as a foreign language. The aim is not only to cater to the multi-layered learners of Chinese in the Australian context, but also in the global environment (Moloney & Xu, 2015a). Based on these dominant influences, it is exceptionally crucial for the native speakers of Chinese as CFL teacher-researchers to understand the local students' school-based and extracurricular life experiences, as well as their existing learning experiences and knowledge, in order to boost the teachers' self-efficacy in curriculum construction of Chinese language learning for Australian school students.

2.4 Conclusion

Apparently, even though 'children's experience should be the starting point and foundation of the curriculum,' they 'are often ignored, which is a tremendous lost opportunity' (Li, 2017, p.43). That is to say, 'the priority is to employ children's experiences fully when the subject contextualized curriculum links with life' (Li, 2017, p.43). Given the above-mentioned, connecting local school students' everyday sociolinguistic activities and their lived experiences to the content sources of curriculum construction for Chinese language learning in the Australian environment tends to make Chinese a learnable and local language for them (Hedges, Cullen & Jordan, 2011). Moreover, it is emphasised that constructing the curriculum for learning Chinese, especially by drawing on the local marginalised students' knowledge, would stimulate their active engagement in learning Chinese in class, as their identity would be recognised in the school-based community (Zipin, 2013). Therefore, in terms of deciding what to teach local students in Chinese class within the Australian school-related context, the sociolinguistic activities-based approach is adopted in this study, which draws on their daily recurring sociolinguistic activities in school to construct a localised curriculum for their learning and use of Chinese in the local context.

CHAPTER 3

Sociolinguistic Activities-Based Approach to Curriculum Construction for Chinese Language Teaching and Learning

3.1 Sociolinguistics for Language Research

Sociolinguistics is 'an interdisciplinary effort to study language in the context of its use, which is part of a wider movement in the social and behavioural sciences' (Florio-Ruane, 1987, p.186). Sociolinguists study 'the routine speech and actions of people in social groups' (p.186), and try to discover patterns of communication that have functional relevance for those individuals (Florio-Ruane, 1987). It is worth stating that Hymes, an originator of sociolinguistics and a scholar who initially applied it to educational research, particularly focused on schooling practices. In his early work, he shed light on ideas pooled by sociolinguists focusing on a variety of disciplines and professions:

> The fundamental point in common is an understanding of social life as something not given in advance and *a priori*, but as having an ineradicable aspect of being constituted by its participants in an ongoing, evolving way. Those who accept this point can agree on giving priority to discovery of what is actually done in local settings and of what it means to participants. The concomitant of that

priority is an empowering of participants as sources of knowledge. (1980, p.xiv, italics added).

According to Hymes, sociolinguistics is an area that is imbued with potentially educational values for interdisciplinary knowledge grabbers in terms of sources of academic content and specific subject knowledge. This enables learners' stored information to be activated for mastering other knowledge from different disciplines. Such a conception supplies educators of cross-subjects with an alternative angle and way of being well-informed, helping them select learning topics and teaching pedagogies for a certain subject field, adjusting them to suit different students' learning expectations and capabilities (McKay, 2017). As for teachers, engaging with sociolinguistic knowledge from their pupils would require examining specific subject knowledge, properly harnessing it in their teaching practices, and then extending the teaching to wider learning contexts in the future (Verhoeven, 1998).

Furthermore, the concept of the 'speech community,' by its very nature, provides a social routine for people who study, work, and live together to get to know each other, and makes daily actual situations happen regularly through the use of their common linguistic terms (Hymes, 1977). Based on this notion, a classroom can be seen as a concrete speech community in which instructors would know what to teach in a learnable style, and thereby pupils would know how to learn in an enjoyable way through the handy observations of the routine talk and daily activities which occur there (Florio-Ruane, 1987). What is more, under the impact of sociolinguistic reform since the 1970s, the progressive concept of Communicative Language Teaching (CLT) has been developed as a basic principle and approach for constructing a curriculum and language teaching to recognise and produce instructive materials, focused on learners' perspectives, for cultivating their communicative competencies in using target language within their real-life situations (Street & Leung, 2010). In this new era, the role of sociolinguistics is endowed with a deeper function that has immersed it into multi-faceted educational fields, especially in language acquisition, which is generally understood as 'the study of social aspects of language as well as the interaction of language with sociocultural and political structures and phenomena,' and 'has much to offer to heritage language

(HL) educators' (Leeman & Serafini, 2016, p.56). Accordingly, sociolinguistics is embedded in heritage language and second language teaching and learning, as it is abundant with valuable knowledge sources for boosting the development of language education (Leeman & Serafini, 2016). Considering the aforementioned, it is clear that sociolinguistics is like a 'reservoir' which is continuously 'filled in' by discursive linguistic repertoires through the interplay with diverse authenticity-oriented social practices, while unceasingly 'pouring out' schooling resources and instruction pedagogies informed by those sociolinguistic activities (Street & Leung, 2010; Duff, 2010; Yiakoumetti, 2012; McKay, 2017). Therefore, how to initiate and utilise such efficacy and popularity specified by sociolinguistic activities, to generate learning resources from such real sociocultural contexts for educational research, particularly for foreign/second language learning, is to be reviewed in the ensuing section.

3.2 Sociolinguistic Activities for Foreign/Second Language Learning

Originally, the term 'sociolinguistic activity' probes into the regular discourse pattern generally used by a particular cohort of people in real-world social happenings, thus focusing on the study of language use and function in reality (Florio-Ruane, 1987). The worth and aptness of sociolinguistics for language education lie in its contribution to generating a series of authentic linguistics-related activities as instructional materials for L2 learning, which can help to overcome the sterility incurred by generic and dead textbooks which ignore culture-specific and localised differences among diverse learners (McKay & Bokhorst-Heng, 2008). Another aspect worth noting is that sociolinguistic activities as the 'facilitator' immersed into EFL (English as a Foreign Language) teaching practices, contributes to making the language attainment process happen through the capturing of, and interplay with, the learning content from real-life experiences (Morton, 2013). However, by its very necessity, the sociolinguistic tactic of selecting language learning materials needs to be encultured and re-adjusted to particularise learners' specific learning desires and capabilities in different educational districts, thereby offsetting the deficit from over-dependency on the ready-produced course book resources (Morton, 2013).

Currently, it is not surprising to find out that using a sociolinguistic perspective to choose and design content sources and learning tasks for EFL textbooks is favoured by more non-English speaking Asian countries, such as China and Vietnam. One reason for this preference is that it is productive to cultivate learners' communicative competencies through exposing them to such tangible learning and using experiences of the target language accompanied by its adapted culture within those learners' own cultural circles (Yuan,et al., 2015; Dang & Seals, 2018). Therefore, one purpose in adopting various sociolinguistic activities as learning content sources is to encourage the authenticity of knowledge delivered in the classroom, which is acceptable and suitable for those foreign/second language learners with diversified sociocultural and linguistic characteristics (van Compernolle, 2016).

Being grounded in such perceptions, the authenticity of language learning materials has a tendency to be regarded as being contextually utilised by conducting corresponding daily localised practices in L2 classrooms (Diao, 2016; van Compernolle & McGregor, 2016). Sociolinguistic activities engender authenticity in the following two ways. Firstly, 'sociolinguistic agency' (p.63) is reconciled by a learner's existing knowledge concerning the perceptible constructs of meaningful linguistic terms in a particular community, namely the authenticity of linguistic relevance and cultural appropriateness (van Compernolle, 2016). Secondly, it is facilitated by a learner's insight to deliberately generate meanings in the course of carrying out those real and existing sociolinguistic activities in that community, being reflected in the formation of authenticity (van Compernolle, 2016).

Correspondingly, considering sociolinguistics as a bond which associates various social practices with real linguistic forms and usages, language educators and researchers have transferred their attention to making foreign/second language teaching more focused on learners' daily sociolinguistic activities for producing authentic learning materials and textbook resources to cater for their differentiated needs. As Abrams and Schiestl (2017) have criticised, the absence of authentic instructional stuff for constructing German curricula failed to achieve the purpose

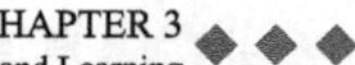

of situation-based application of the learned knowledge for American students. Such a concern was engendered from the gap between the existing standardised German textbooks in the U.S., and the special deviations the students adapted from their real-life L2 learning experiences. Meanwhile, Allehyani, Burnapp, and Wilson (2017) investigated several Saudi Arabian English educators' responses and awareness towards selecting and utilising materials for teaching EFL from their nationalised textbooks, instead of authentic learning resources. The study found that these practitioners of English teaching strongly held a positive attitude to employing such authenticity-based learning material in relation to local students' cultural preferences, thus enhancing their interactive proficiency in daily life. Similarly, Castillo Losada, Insuasty, and Jaime Osorio (2017) identified the major functions and influences of using authentic learning materials and tasks on students' academic achievements and teachers' professional enactments. On the one hand, in terms of the students' learning benefits, they were naturally endowed with more opportunities for concrete contact with the target language through being involved in contextualised learning activities in class, as their learning interest and eagerness were sustained regardless of whether the learners had low or high levels of language capability. On the other hand, as English language teachers their courses were equipped with a certain cultural and linguistic richness, and their practical teaching experiences were enriched, even though they needed to spend extra time deciding on the authenticity and appropriateness of those potential teaching content sources, and transferring those elements to the process of course implementation. Enhancing the linguistic learnability of content sources for language curriculum called for well-selected authentic resources with cultural appropriateness. For instance, it has also been argued that such genuine learning material can broaden and deepen language learners' exposure to and understanding of real-life linguistic and sociocultural features from the target language community (Ahmed, 2017). In doing so, it would not only improve students' communicative skills in real contexts to serve a specific purpose, but also enable them to discover more novel linguistic expressions through performing those authenticity-oriented learning activities in the target language (Ozverir, Osam & Herrington, 2017).

Accordingly, seeking sociolinguistic activities-based instruction content becomes the priority when making Chinese language education available worldwide, which goes beyond the conventional textbooks whose designs are based on the native Chinese learners' needs and particularities (Duff et al., 2013). This main concern is linked to Pennycook's notion (2010) that language is an embodiment of social practice, thereby facilitating the production of teaching and learning resources from daily situated sociolinguistic activities. Likewise, in order to make Chinese learnable for Australian local school children, Singh and Han (2014) proposed a novel perspective: To make full use of their daily recurrent sociolinguistic activities in school as a 'mediator' to construct suitable Chinese learning content and instruction strategies. This process can transfer these learners' existing linguistic knowledge from English used for conducting those Australian culture-oriented activities, to their learning of Chinese. Here, it is worth stating that the sociolinguistic activities adopted are specifically defined as Australian local school students' recurrent doings undertaken in English in the school-based community for effecting their daily communication and learning practices within such an English-speaking educational setting (Carter, 2006; Kelly, 2012; Singh & Han, 2014).

3.3 Conclusion

Learning content plays a dominant role in the process of constructing a curriculum for Chinese language education, especially in crafting appropriate Chinese textbooks from the perspective of Australian school students (Moloney & Xu, 2015b; Scrimgeour, Foster & Mao, 2013). Also, to promote more fruitful learning outcomes of Chinese within the Australian sociocultural environment, it is necessary for native Chinese teachers to recognise the local school students' preferences and habits towards the instruction content and methods in mastering Chinese through engaging in intercultural awareness regarding choices of proper pedagogy (Moloney, 2013; Moloney & Xu, 2015a). As already mentioned, in terms of cultivating the learners' communicative competencies, language educators prefer to start with the sociolinguistic perspective to explore, discover, and generate learning content from the learners' daily authentic activities, especially when

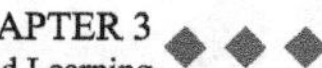

teaching English as a foreign/second language in the classroom.

Nevertheless, there exists little literature concerning how authentic learning materials from those localised sociolinguistic practices of non-native Chinese learners contribute to the formation of appropriate and learnable textbook resources for Chinese language curricula. Therefore, the sociolinguistic activities-based approach is seen as both a trend and an antidote, which can be conducive to repositioning learning content sources of curriculum construction for Chinese language teaching in the Australian educational environment. In addition, it is contributory to re-shaping the identities of local school students due to the prioritised role of deciding on their favoured learning topics from familiar and age-proper sociolinguistic activities. That is to say, the students' daily recurring sociolinguistic activities provide the lens for directing Chinese curriculum construction located in the Australian sociocultural context, with regard to what constitutes local students' expected and desired learning content and instruction styles that can maintain their interest, as well as boost their sense of achievement in learning Chinese.

In order to make such learning resources from the students' everyday recurrent sociolinguistic happenings entirely deployable for their learning of Chinese, the literature regarding the student-centred pedagogy is going to be illustrated and elucidated upon in the following section, namely as to how the native teacher-researcher can better engage the local children in Chinese learning within the school-based community.

CHAPTER 4

Student-Centred Pedagogy as a 'Remedy' for Knowing Australian Local School Students

Teachers tend to choose what and how to teach based on students' interests and their existing knowledge when adopting the student-centred pedagogy in language teaching (Nunan, 1988). It is crucial for language instructors to regard their students as intellectuals and seriously take their prior learning experiences into consideration (Graff, 2001). Consequently, student-centred pedagogy provides learners with collective and supportive learning opportunities which will allow them to actively engage in the language classroom (Mahendra, et al., 2005). Furthermore, as Lindquist(2010) indicates, knowing students means not only understanding their literacy learning experiences, but also being able to conjecture what is in jeopardy for them during the process of making different pedagogical connections. Accordingly, the student-centred pedagogy is beneficial for the mutual generation of learning content, as well as choosing appropriate teaching methods when students are being situated in such a tailored and compatible learning environment.

From the perspective of student-centred pedagogy, students themselves, not lecturers, play an important role in designing an engaging framework and creating individual learning modules. Meanwhile, students regard themselves as active mediators in constructing a portrayal of their expected learning content for curricula, which promotes the co-production of course content and course organisation (Orr,

Yorke & Blair, 2014). In student-centred pedagogy, the teacher is regarded as a facilitator for students' exploration of unknown knowledge. It is anticipated that the facilitator will pinpoint students' existing capacities so that supportive learning opportunities will be available for them in class (Altinyelken, 2011). That is to say, when it comes to the impacts of student-centred pedagogy on innovative classroom practices, the pedagogy is endowed with new features and approaches that enable students to enjoy their learning in the form of some entertaining activities, such as drawing, singing, drama performing and game playing (Altinyelken, 2011). As a result, 'knowing the students' will make their ideas transparent, rather than make their ideas 'buried treasure.' This type of information can not only help teachers discover the core suppositions that commonly exist in their students' demands and thoughts, but also assist teachers in selecting learning tasks and designing learning activities that are, to a large extent, suitable for diverse students (Smith, 2000). Therefore, the student-centred pedagogy, as a tour guide, leads the native teacher-researcher to have a better understanding of the Australian students, including their preferred instruction strategies and methods in mastering Chinese in the local school-based community. Then, such learner-directed instruction strategies developed from the student-centred pedagogy are to be adjusted and adapted to suit the Australian school students' learning styles, as well as to justify their effectiveness in making Chinese learnable for the students within the local education system and environment.

CHAPTER 5

Language as a Local Practice

Chapters 5, 6, and 7 focus on constructing a theoretic-pedagogical framework to investigate Australian students' various embodiments of their daily recurring sociolinguistic activities that they perform in English, and their preferred learning habits in the school-based community for developing a localised, learnable, and student-centred Chinese curriculum in the local education milieu. On the one hand, this research project is targeted at making Chinese a localised language for Australian local school students through observing and noting the everyday regular happenings from their familiar situations. On the other hand, to make full use of the localised learning resources, it aims to discover and adapt appropriate instruction strategies from the students' perspectives to further improve the learnability of Chinese in the local context. In doing so, the process for converging conceptual constructs begins with paying heed to Pennycook's notion (2010) of 'language as a local practice' for looking at second/foreign language teaching and learning used here to refer to teaching Chinese as a second language to emergent language learners from an alternative perspective, namely transferring our understanding of language from being a static entity to being a dynamic process (e.g. languaging and translanguaging).

Following such a shift, flexible and ecological pedagogy approaches are employed in Chinese language teaching, including creating situated language learning for effecting the students' legitimate peripheral participation (LPP)[1] in the learning community of Chinese language practices based on their localised social practices (Lave & Wenger, 1991).

5.1 Shifting from Language to Languaging and Translanguaging

The following section is mainly concerned with the exploration of Pennycook's (2010) notion of 'language as a local practice' as the departure point to make sense of how to effect language as embodiments of multiple local practices. The consideration of such a concept is specifically located within the field of Chinese language education in the Australian school-based context.

The debates between 'language as a system of signs' (e.g. Saussure and Chomsky), which 'removes language from the context of use,' as well as 'language as action' (e.g. Bakhtin and Vološinov), which 'proposes dialogic position on language' and 'acquires life in concrete verbal communication rather than the abstract linguistic system of language forms' have evolved into the corresponding arguments shifting from language to language use in reality, termed as 'languaging,' and then followed by 'translanguaging' (Jørgensen, 2008; Pennycook, 2010; García & Wei, 2014, p.7).

The notion of languaging originally derives from the theory of autopoiesis suggested by the Chilean biologists Humberto Maturana and Francisco Varela in 1973. They contend that human beings' experiences make up the attainment and construction of necessary knowledge, which is attached to the enactment of those take-it-for-granted actions and practices in the real world (Maturana & Varela, 1992). In addition, according to Maturana and Varela (1992), 'all doing is knowing, and all knowing is doing' (p.26), which is further explained as follows:

1 Legitimate peripheral participation is mainly concerned with 'the process by which newcomers become part of a community of practice' (Lave & Wenger, 1991, p.29). Specifically speaking, it refers to the process whereby 'a person's intentions to learn are engaged and the meaning of learning is configured through the process of becoming a full participant in a sociocultural practice' (Lave & Wenger, 1991, p.29). By doing so, that 'provides a way to speak about the relations between newcomers and old-timers, and about activities, identities, artifacts, and communities of knowledge and practice' (Lave & Wenger, 1991, p.29).

> It is by languaging that the act of knowing, in the behavioural coordination, which is language, brings forth a world. We work out our lives in a mutual linguistic coupling, not because language permits us to reveal ourselves but because we are constituted in language in a continuous becoming that we bring forth with others (pp.234-235).

This implies that languaging regards language as a dynamic process in people's daily lives rather than as a static entity. It is presumed that 'language is an everyday phenomenon which is used, constructed, and ascribed meaning in the local realities and encounters of people,' which is, in turn, beneficial for facilitating 'further developments and communicative encounters' (Karrebæk, Madsen & Møller, 2015, p.2). In view of that, languaging is thereby an elaborated jargon used to characterise and 'capture an ongoing process that is always being created as we interact with the world lingually' (García & Wei, 2014, p.8). It follows that languaging occurs as a natural phenomenon as people are intertwined in social interplay.

However, when it comes to 'languaging,' there are a few divergences according to different fields to which it is being applied. For instance, Halliday (1985) adapts the term 'languaging' to identify 'how people exchange meanings' through engaging 'a semiotic system,' 'a systematic resource for meaning' (p.7) in real situations. Being such a linguistic perspective, it is assumed that languaging becomes a medium for human beings to interpret and understand the actual world as they enact a series of concrete activities (Lankiewicz, 2014). Additionally, in terms of languaging, linguistic features are considered as very essential constituents, as they 'appear in the shape of units and regularities' that 'are also associated with values, meanings, speakers, places, etc.' for the purpose of mastering a new language in real life (Jørgensen & Juffermans, as cited in Lankiewicz, 2014, p.2). Consequently, it is claimed that 'languaging is that people do not normally speak a language but rather actively employ their linguistic predisposition – languaging' (Lankiewicz, 2014, p.2), which echoes Mignolo's statement (1996) that 'languages are conceived and languaging is practiced' (p.181). People's languaging aptitude is not necessarily dependent on the presence of Universal Grammar, as proposed by Chomsky, due to the real bond between the form and the meaning (Lankiewicz, 2014).

Languaging is a popular concept in the arena of language instruction. For example, as indicated by Swain (2005), the role of 'output' in second language learning lies in its generation of the target language via 'practising,' which shifts the course of meaning production from 'a thing, or a product' to 'an action, or a process' (p.471). Furthermore, Swain (2006) articulates that languaging is embodied via the 'coming-to-know-while-speaking phenomenon' (later termed as 'talking-it-through') that 'serves as a vehicle through which thinking is articulated and transformed into an artifactual form' (p.97). That is to say, 'languaging is a process which creates a visible or audible product about which one can language further' (Swain, 2006, p.97). At the same time, speaking of 'languaging' as it occurs during the process of second/ foreign language teaching and learning, its hidden worth and potential importance are explained as follows:

> Languaging refers to the process of making meaning and shaping knowledge and experience through language. It is part of what constitutes learning. Languaging about language is one of the ways we learn language. This means that the languaging (the dialogue or private speech) about language that learners engage in takes on new significance. In it, we can observe learners operating on linguistic data and coming to an understanding of previously less well-understood material. In languaging, we see learning taking place (Swain, 2006, p.98).

Therefore, it is stressed that language learners' languaging, on the one hand, works as the catalyst to convey and convert their abstract linguistic mindset into a tangible practice. And on the other hand, languaging plays a positive function in promoting language learners' generation of novel senses and understandings of L2 mastery, thereby building a bridge to connect the concrete learning experiences and the conceptualised language knowledge (Swain, 2006).

What is more, it is debatable whether 'languaging is not simply a vehicle for communication, but plays critical roles in creating, transforming, and augmenting higher mental processes' (Swain & Lapkin, 2011, p.106). This debate concerns Vygotsky's stance (1962) regarding the internal relationship between language and cognitive processes. As noted by Vygotsky (1962), 'thought is not merely expressed in words; it comes into existence through them' (p.125). He says that 'thought undergoes many changes as it turns into speech. It does not merely find expression in speech; it finds its reality and form' (Vygotsky, 1962, p.126). Informed by this point of view, Smagorinsky (1998) puts forward that applying such didactic tactics as the 'speech and speech-based activities' (p.172) to language learning tends to make mental processes 'articulated, transformed into an artifactual form, and then available as a source of further reflection,' because thinking enacted in the process of speaking becomes 'an agent in the production of meaning' (p.173).

Despite the fact that such an internalised mechanism happens naturally and as expected in the process of languaging, it is worth noting that languaging is 'not just a brain dump' or 'communicating' (Swain & Lapkin, 2011, p.105). It is 'an essential process inherent in positive cognitive change' (p.106) and 'adds to the meaning of communication the power of language to mediate attention, recall, and knowledge creation' (p.107), eventually achieving thinking through languaging (Swain & Lapkin, 2011). In summary, from the perspective of sociolinguistics, especially for second/foreign language learning, languaging is 'perceived as a continuum or more appropriately as a cline (to account for its multidimensional fractal nature, as opposed to the flatness embedded in the notion of a continuum) of meaning-making resulting from the potential inscribed in linguistic systems' (Lankiewicz, 2014, p.14).

Drawing on the notion of languaging, translanguaging emerges as an innovative outlook and an ecological approach to second language acquisition (Leather & van Dam, 2003; van Lier, 2004). Originally, in the educational context translanguaging is identified as 'a pedagogical practice where students are asked to alternate languages for the purposes of receptive or productive use' (García & Wei, 2014, p.20). In an extended sense, translanguaging can be referred to as 'both the complex language practices of plurilingual individuals and communities, as well as the pedagogical approaches that use those complex practices,' and as 'the product of acting and languaging in our highly technological globalized world' (García & Wei, 2014, p.20). At the same time, when it comes to definitions and understandings on translanguaging, different scholars tend to have diversified views. A case in point is Canagarajah's argument (2011) that translanguaging is the embodiment of 'the ability of multilingual speakers to shuttle between languages, treating the diverse languages that form their repertoire as an integrated system' (p.401). Such an angle thus contributes to developing various instruction practices from the approaches that are formed and retained through multilingual learners' own funds of knowledge, which are effective both for themselves and others (Canagarajah, 2011). Baker provides another perspective as the first scholar to provide a translation of 'translanguaging' from the Welsh. From his perspective, translanguaging means 'the process of making meaning, shaping experiences, gaining understanding and knowledge through the use of two languages' (Baker, 2011, p.288). Correspondingly, to distinguish the notion of 'languaging' from 'translanguaging,' different scholars have made various efforts to make clear sense between them. Such as García (2009) who described translanguaging as:

> The language practices of bilinguals from the perspective of the users themselves, and not simply describing bilingual language use or bilingual contact from the perspective of the language itself, the language practices of bilinguals are examples of what we are here calling *translanguaging*... For us, translanguagings are *multiple discursive practices* in which bilinguals engage in order to *make sense of their bilingual worlds* (p.45, italics added).

In addition, as informed by Wei (2011), such a phenomenon is characterised as follows:

> Translanguaging is both going between different linguistic structures and systems, including different modalities (speaking, writing, signing, listening, reading, remembering) and going beyond them. It includes the full range of linguistic performances of multilingual language users for purposes that transcend the combination of structures, the alternation between systems, the transmission of information, and the representation of values, identities, and relationships. The act of translanguaging then is transformative in nature; it creates a social space for the multilingual language user by bringing together different dimensions of their personal history, experience and environment, their attitude, beliefs and ideology, their cognitive and physical capacity into one coordinated and meaningful performance, and make it into a lived experience (p.1223).

Subsequently, to advance the application of translanguaging to the specific classroom context, it is pointed out that 'translanguaging entails using one language to reinforce the other in order to increase understanding and in order to augment the pupil's ability in both languages' (Williams, as cited in Lewis, Jones & Baker, 2012a, p.644). Further explanation is provided:

> Translanguaging tries to draw on all the linguistic resources of the child to maximise understanding and achievement. Thus, both languages are used in a dynamic and functionally integrated manner to organise and mediate mental processes in understanding, speaking, literacy, and, not least, learning (Lewis, Jones & Baker, 2012b, p.655).

More specifically, when translanguaging is introduced into language education, it is confronted with such situations as dynamic bilingualism (Lewis, Jones & Baker, 2012b). According to García (2009), in both physical and visual senses 'dynamic bilingualism' suggests that learners should be equipped with 'differentiated abilities and uses of multiple languages' (p.54) in terms of language use in the new era. That phenomenon reflects 'a general and holistic concept of which translanguaging is a process' (Lewis, Jones & Baker, 2012b, p.656). Similarly, the term 'emergent bilinguals' also labels the vibrant and diverse essence of students' bilingual practices (García & Kleifgen, 2010; Sayer, 2013; Gort & Sembiante, 2015).

Given the very nature of translanguaging as it occurs in the language classroom, the corresponding teaching strategies have been put forward to fully exploit learners' potential bilingual competencies in meaning-making. Creese and Blackledge (2010) propose a flexible bilingual pedagogy, which 'adopts a translanguaging approach and is used by participants for identity performance as well as the business of language learning and teaching' (p.112). Such a bilingual pedagogical belief highlights the synthesis of languages for teaching and learning, as opposed to the separation between them, thus integrating students' linguistic and cultural repertoires from their daily lives (Creese & Blackledge, 2010; Creese & Blackledge, 2011; Gort & Sembiante, 2015). Accompanied by the flexible bilingual pedagogy, another perspective concerns language ecology (Leather & van Dam, 2003; Creese & Blackledge, 2010; Gort & Sembiante, 2015). This perspective is primarily involved with 'the study of diversity within specific socio-political settings in which the processes of language use create, reflect, and challenge particular hierarchies and hegemonies, however transient these might be' (Creese & Blackledge, 2010, p.104). To be precise, ecological tactics make it possible for teachers to link students' gained language to their mastery of novel language knowledge (van Lier, 2008).

Ecological language awareness is beneficial for creating a 'panoramic space' in which 'perception and action go together' by means of 'sustaining a rich multisensory experience of, in and with language,' therefore 'providing the conditions for emergent learning' (van Lier, 2008, pp.54-55). An ecological position on translanguaging not only facilitates young language learners to be creative and dynamic bilingual producers, but also inspires them to receive new information from their evolving bilingual inventories (Wells, 1986; Gort & Sembiante, 2015). Accordingly, it is claimed that 'such ecological models acknowledge that bilinguals' languaging practices are dynamic, malleable, and influenced by naturalistic opportunities in the environment that tap into their potential to develop and use multiple languages, language varieties, and literacies' (Gort & Sembiante, 2015, p.9).

The concept of languaging has an emphasis on the local students' daily social practices, in particular for their learning of Chinese in the Australian context, because they are empowered to make sense of their own learning from real-world situations by virtue of being engaged in their familiar sociolinguistic activities. The notion of translanguaging as a mediated mechanism offers a flexible and ecological approach for teaching Chinese to the English-monolingual learners through enacting their emergent bilingualism and discursive language practices. These two major shifts concerning Chinese language teaching and learning in the local school-based community provide innovative visions for effecting the Chinese languaging process, and mobilising their translanguaging capabilities, by means of adopting suitable learning content and multi-layered instruction strategies from these young Chinese learners.

5.2 Situated Learning

Language education has experienced a pedagogical turn from the originally static 'language' teaching to such dynamic learning processes as 'languaging,' subsequently followed by 'translanguaging' from a flexible and ecological perspective. Meanwhile, when it comes to 'language as a local practice':

> This refers not only to the ways in which language use must always be related to *place*, must always be understood in terms of its *embeddedness in locality*, but also to the ways in which any understanding of the *locality of language* must also encompass an appreciation of the *locality of perspective*, of the different ways in which *language, locality and practice* are conceived in different contexts (Pennycook, 2010, p.4, italics added).

Such a statement provides a range of hints concerning how to transform the static language teaching into a dynamic and active learning process from two dimensions. One emphasis is placed on the specific 'locality-place(s)' for using language in reality. Another emphasis is attached to the 'practice-doing(s)' for making such language use become concrete actions in various situations.

This provides some insights for the field of Chinese language education with regard to making the learning and use of Chinese specifically located in diversified situations through the enactment of embodied social activities when considering the reclaimed place and space. Correspondingly, the following section explains various viewpoints regarding the situated learning practices.

Initially, according to Hanks (1991), situated learning focuses on 'the relationship between learning and social situations in which it occurs' in order to 'explore the situated character of human understanding and communication' (p.14). It is then argued that 'learning is a process that takes place in a participation framework, not in an individual mind,' which is closely tied to 'actional contexts' rather than 'self-contained structures' (Hanks, 1991, p.15). That is to say, social activities can create an appropriate environment for making learning process happen in such actual situations from daily life, thus equipping people with certain behaviour patterns and expertise (Lave & Wenger, 1991). In addition, according to the model of legitimate peripheral participation the learner is treated as 'a legitimate peripheral participant interacting with masterful speakers' through engaging in daily happenings (Hanks, 1991, p.19).

Being grounded in this perspective, Chinese language learning is not simply 'situated in practice — as if it were some independently reifiable process that just happened to be located somewhere,' it is also 'an integral part of generative social practice in the lived-in world' (Lave & Wenger, 1991, p.35). As the learning process is characterised with such dynamic and authentic 'situatedness,' to capture those re-situated social activities in the local Chinese classroom becomes the new trend, and the main objective of Chinese language teaching and learning based on the flexible and ecological pedagogy choices in reality.

The learned Chinese language knowledge tends to be movable and sustainable through enacting the practical legitimate peripheral participation during the process of situated learning. It is therefore worth mentioning that the sustainability for language learning means:

> Reviewing past language practices to meet the needs of the present while not compromising those of future generations. Thus, the sustainability of languaging is a *new* copy of the past, a dynamic relocalization in space and time, a fertile performative mimesis that brings us to a creative emergence, a new and generative becoming (García, as cited in García & Wei, 2014, p.72, italics added).

This also opens up the possibility of connecting the local students' daily school-based social practices to their attainment of new Chinese language knowledge in a collective and interactive manner in class, namely acquiring the Chinese language by performing actions in the real social context. That eventually is beneficial for these young Chinese learners in mapping their learning process, constructing their identity, as well as maintaining their involvement in Chinese language learning when positioning themselves within the structure of legitimate peripheral participation. Therefore, the relationship between the 'newcomers' (not well-engaged learners) and 'old-timers' (language experts) in Chinese class is constructed to be supportive and collaborative, progressively developing a sustainable continuum vis-à-vis being enabled and located in the mastery and application of Chinese language knowledge in their tangible and mutual social practices, instead of in discrete personal engagement.

5.3 Social Practices for Languaging and Translanguaging

According to Pennycook (2010), 'practices are not just things we do, but rather bundles of activities that are the central organisation of social life' (p.2). Languaging occurs as 'part of a multifaceted interplay between humans and the world' (Pennycook, 2010, p.2). In this sense, people's doing or even singing are regarded as common practices in daily life (Pennycook, 2010). Meanwhile, the accompanying social activities from such everyday happenings that embody the languaging process (language use), as well as the situation (locality) in which they take place (Pennycook, 2010). Consequently, looking at 'language as a local practice' (languaging process) 'takes us away from a notion of language as a pre-given entity that may be used in a location,' while leading us to delve into 'language as part of diverse social activity' (Pennycook, 2010, p.2).

The notion of 'language as a local practice' guides us to look at the mediated social activities from various real-world contexts used for practising language, thus implying the internal connection between space and place for the localising (locality) of a language (Pennycook, 2010). Importantly, to be a localised process it necessarily involves local practices due to their significance in constructing locality (Pennycook, 2010). Therefore, the notions of languaging and translanguaging help us build a direction 'towards an understanding of language as a product of the embodied social practices that bring it about' (Pennycook, 2010, p.9).

In this regard, various forms of people's regular activities that are rooted in their everyday social practices are labelled with such locatedness to a large extent considering the specific place and space. Particularly, the Australian localised social practices from this school-based community are to be adapted as a bridge for crafting the situated language learning in Chinese class. That is to say, it not only ushers in the exploration of the dynamic and interactive process of languaging, given the diversified localities and students' doings in such places, but also accommodates the flexible and ecological translanguaging pedagogical beliefs regarding Chinese language education as more and more bilingual or multilingual students are emerging from the local Chinese classroom. The next section sheds light on the conditions and possibilities for constructing a translanguaging space to gather and distribute such cultural and linguistic repertoires, which can be utilised as a vehicle for effecting languaging process for Chinese language teaching and learning in a way which is mutually and equally dialogic between teacher and students.

CHAPTER 6

Constructing a Translanguaging Space

As highlighted by García and Wei (2014), creating a space for performing translanguaging, especially in language education, is conducive to inviting such ecological and sustainable L2 language pedagogy into a democratic schooling structure, as students' agency is prioritised and activated to 'negotiate their linguistic and meaning-making repertoires' (p.75). In doing so, an equal and shared dialogic space between instructors and learners is established to ensure the information is exchanged in a bilateral pattern rather than a unilateral one.

6.1 Negotiable Structure for Mobilising Students' Agency

From a sociological perspective, the interrelationship between structure on the one hand, and teacher and students' agency on the other, is a recurrent issue for educational research. Both macro-level and micro-level forces of structure and agency shape educational change (Stromquist, 2015). 'Structure' is the systematic configurations that can both empower and restrain individual actions, through which people appreciate how things ought to be completed, practised and systematised around those identifications and competencies that support those appreciations (Rigby, Woulfin & März, 2016). 'Agency' refers to 'people's ability to make choices, to take control, self-regulate, and thereby pursue their goals as individuals leading, potentially, to personal or social transformation' (Duff, 2012, p.417). To be exact, agency designates positioned practices, or the progressive ability of individuals to take actions (Rigby, Woulfin & März, 2016). Agency is thus a vital facet for a foreign/second language learner which can have an in-depth influence on how he/she begins to learn and interact in the target language community (Duff et al., 2013). Investigating the interaction between structure and agency is really a rewarding subject during the process of implementing government policy regarding the local (second/foreign) language(s) education, which is mainly concerned with the intricate structures, multifaceted stakeholders, as well as the necessity for enduring the development of local education (Rigby, Woulfin & März, 2016). Awareness of the integration of structure and agency ensures that teacher-researchers have better understandings of the educational policy implementation concerning language teaching and learning in the local school-based community.

Furthermore, from a sociocultural angle, the 'immediate environment' (p.100) offers students the necessary conditions for their learning in which they act as the 'agent(s)' (p.100) who have the power to 'perceive, analyse, reject or accept solutions offered, make decisions' (p.101) on their own (Swain, 2006). By doing so, this encourages second/foreign language learners to mobilise their 'prior knowledge' (Swain, 2006, p.101) for developing novel language knowledge in an emancipated learning process. Nevertheless, students can be easily regarded as 'puppets' who are merely operated by structural power due to their ignored agency, choices or actions through the process of exploring their learning experiences (Rind, 2016). Structural power has an in-depth influence on the variables in education, such as teaching strategies, assessment methods, curriculum construction, physical space and students' learning experiences (Rind, 2016). Consequently, teachers' agency and students' agency are both influenced by macro and micro structural forces, including the educational policies of the government, the national and state curriculum requirements, as well as the specified lesson plans of a local school. Such structural factors can lead to impaired interactions between teachers' agency and students' agency. Specifically, on the one hand it means that students can have no power or actions in negotiating and selecting the content sources for curriculum construction.

On the other hand, teaching practices are controlled and influenced by such macro and micro structural forces.

In this research project, structure refers to the existing state syllabus and national curriculum for the Australian students' learning of Chinese in the local school-based community where the Chinese teacher-researcher is based for constructing daily lesson plans. In this project, the local students' agency is empowered and emancipated to the maximum degree in terms of deciding on their preferred learning content and tasks, as well as appropriate instruction styles and activities within the structure of the Chinese classroom in this school. Subsequently, it captures the notion of 'community of practice' in a way which supplements the structure and agency standpoint regarding the local students' learning of Chinese in the school-based community.

6.2 Community of Practice for Knowledge Co-Construction

The concept of community, along with the concept of identity has been well-defined in many diverse ways. Lave and Wenger (1991) were cognitive anthropologists who developed the concept of 'community of practice' (CoP). It is an approach that takes both structure and agency into account with reference to conceptualising the community. 'Community of practice' is described as 'groups of people who share a concern, a set of problems, or a passion about a topic, and who deepen their knowledge and expertise in this area by interacting on an ongoing basis' (Wenger, McDermott & Snyder, 2002, p.9). Learning is more than the process of acquiring definite forms of knowledge, and the circumstances of co-participation need to be placed into such a process to socialise relationships (Lave & Wenger, 1991). It also requires that group involvement in learning occurs, based on the appropriate existing milieu (Lave & Wenger, 1991). Hence, learners are not considered as the persons who merely obtain the existing knowledge paradigm through the perspective from which they understand the world, but also through the progress they make as they engage in the knowledge structures they have constructed.

Legitimacy affects the ways learners achieve access to a specific community of practice (Barnawi, 2009). Beginners need to be granted an ample sense of legitimacy to be treated as valuable prospective learners. It is also contended that 'only with legitimacy can all inevitable tumbling and violations become opportunities for learning rather than cause for dismissal, neglect, or exclusion' (Wenger, 1998, p.101). At the same time, as noted by Lave and Wenger (1991) 'the development of identity' (p.115) is a dominant aspect of novices' legitimate peripheral participation in a community of practice. In this sense, 'learning and a sense of identity are inseparable' (p.115), which is similar to 'a reciprocal relation' (p.116) between learners and their language practices in a community (Lave & Wenger, 1991). Therefore, legitimacy acts as an indispensable role in the process of language teaching and learning due to its enablement of access to the learners' agency. The more advanced the level of legitimacy which is bestowed upon the learners in a classroom context, the more they are willing to transfer and build their identity in the community of practice (Toohey, 2000).

These young learners build distinctly social and cultural identities within the local Chinese classroom. The Chinese classroom is regarded as a vital place where local school students gain Chinese language knowledge, such as linguistic and cultural capabilities within an instructional environment. As a result, it is crucial for students to engage in classroom activities to obtain such competencies (Barnawi, 2009; Hirst, 2007; Morita, 2004). Further, it is valuable to have an in-depth understanding that 'the membership and identities that the students constructed in a given classroom simultaneously shaped and were shaped by their class participation,' because such 'dynamic co-construction of identity and participation also suggests that negotiating identity is situated' (Morita, 2004, p.596). That correspondingly requires that the learning community of Chinese language practices should be established in the local school-based milieu. In doing so, these local students' identities in learning a new language — Chinese, are potentially enacted and constructed through involving them in the learning content and activities embedded in their daily social practices and educational traditions.

However, most educational research employs teachers' standpoints to recognise student-teacher interactions in the L2 learning classroom. Here, the Chinese teacher-researcher adopts the notion 'community of practice' to capture the dynamic interaction between the local students' agency and the negotiable structure in the Chinese classroom from the students' perspective. This means the focus is on how the students mutually negotiate to generate their preferred topics and content for constructing a learnable Chinese curriculum in such a dialogic learning community. That echoes the notion of 'co-learning' which occurs in bilingual or multilingual classrooms, where 'multiple agents simultaneously try to adapt to one another's behaviour so as to produce desirable outcomes that would be shared by the contributing agents' (Wei, 2014, p.169). Such a process lies not merely in requiring the Chinese teacher-researcher to explore the appropriate teaching approaches to 'allow equitable participation for all in the classroom' (Wei, 2014, p.170), but also in enabling the local students to 'build a more genuine community of practice' (Wei, 2014, p.170) for their situated learning of Chinese, as well as allowing the formation and transformation of identity, thereby eventually evolving their 'dynamic and participatory engagement' (Brantmeier, as cited in Wei, 2014, p.170) for the Chinese curriculum co-construction in terms of producing learnable content sources and suitable instruction styles.

Accordingly, the Chinese teacher-researcher develops into the role of 'a learning facilitator, a scaffolder, and a critical reflection enhancer,' whereas the student grows into 'an empowered explorer, a meaning maker, and a responsible knowledge constructor' in Chinese class (Wei, 2014, p.169). As for teaching Chinese as a foreign/second language toemergent language learners, it is pointed out that native Chinese instructors should transition their original pedagogical beliefs in order to achieve the 'mutual adaptation of behaviour' (Wei, 2014, p.169) between teacher and learners, as that is the very essence of co-learning (Moloney & Xu, 2015b). In this sense, the desired knowledge of Chinese language tends to be mutually constructed by these local students and the teacher-researcher in an equally dialogic space, where the real dialogue essentially facilitates the learnable knowledge to be co-produced (Wells, 1999).

CHAPTER 7

Deployment of Students' Funds of Knowledge

'Funds of knowledge' is theoretically underpinned by sociocultural theory (González et al., 2005). In the following section, this is reviewed from two dimensions. One aspect is related to its conceptualised understandings. Another aspect is about its practical applications to educational research.

7.1 The Concept of Funds of Knowledge

'Funds of knowledge' is a concept that means empowering teachers, students, and parents to work together in a (purportedly) liberating pedagogical environment that can redress the unbalanced relations of power in education (González et al., 2005). In particular, this concept concentrates on the poor communities and working-class families that are habitually disregarded in education as sources of valuable knowledge (González et al., 2005). 'Funds of knowledge' develop as families are involved in household activities and interactions with social systems, which takes on a historical depth, a social width, and a conditional nature. The argument is that daily classroom teaching practice can exploit such knowledge to enrich students' engagement, performance and achievement (González et al., 2005). This concept inspires teachers, including pre-service and in-service teachers to enthusiastically utilise the funds of knowledge from students' households and communities during the process of development of educational practice (González et al., 2005). Therefore, the notion of 'funds of knowledge' is defined as 'historically accumulated and culturally developed bodies of knowledge and skills essential for household or individual functioning and well-being' (González et al., 2005, p.72). Here, it is worth mentioning that the local students' funds of knowledge are understood as their knowledge and capabilities in relation to performing their daily sociolinguistic events and learning activities in English, which are picked up and preserved in the school-based community.

7.2 Practical Applications of Funds of Knowledge in Education Context

This section explores the literature on the empirical applications of funds of knowledge tactics in the educational context. Such a pedagogical approach has been of interest for researchers and educators of both literacy and art teaching at the levels of preschool, elementary, and secondary education to improve students' learning achievement.

For example, Kim and Lee (2012) investigated an EFL teacher in R.O. Korea who was utilising students' 'cultural funds of knowledge' to enhance their class participation and engagement. Their research outcomes suggest teachers of language teaching need to appreciate and build on the local students' various funds of knowledge (e.g. culture, languages, and social practices) to develop curricula for second language learning. As local students possess diverse cultural and language backgrounds of their own in a second language teaching and learning context, there exists a gap between the teachers' and students' cultures. Namely, the foreign language teachers as native speakers might not be aware of the local students' cultures and existing knowledge or the worth of them. What is more, quite a few noteworthy pedagogical connections and curriculum content sources from students' interaction with their family members, peers and teachers can provide valuable opportunities to generate their funds of knowledge from the household contexts and community activities, as well as early education surroundings (Hedges, Cullen & Jordan, 2011).

Hence, creating curricula based on students' interests and their corresponding knowledge base is a way for teachers to empower them as positive knowledge constructors rather than passive knowledge recipients.

Teachers are advised to draw on the components of students' funds of knowledge and make genuine assessments via indigenous knowledge systems to restructure evaluation methods and criteria to assess students' advancement in language learning (Coles-Ritchie & Charles, 2011). However, there exist some issues concerning the implementation of indigenised assessment by using students' funds of knowledge, including parents', other teachers', and administrators' oppositions, as well as students' uncertain reaction to the newly-developed assessment system. A curriculum built on the knowledge that is familiar to the students from the marginalised sections of a community arouses their more robust involvement in learning due to its resonance with their cultural identity (Zipin, 2013). On the contrary, the critical voice suggests that socially marginalised learners tend to be alienated from daily school education if the curriculum draws exclusively on the mainstream funds of knowledge and cultural capital of students (Zipin, 2013). It is also contended that teachers' professional education and learning may be more productive if it is based on exploring and evaluating students' funds of knowledge, as well as employing them to cultivate the curriculum construction (Hedges, 2012). It is also suggested that the practical knowledge derived from students' daily sociolinguistic activities can possibly be included inthe research behind curriculum construction, which can support or challenge their own implicit knowledge by means of evidence-informed inquiry (Hedges, 2012).

As for pupils, knowledge cannot be accessed except through 'language practices with which they're already familiar' (García & Wei, 2014, p.80). In turn, 'language practices cannot be developed except through the students' existing knowledge' (García & Wei, 2014, p.80). Such a consideration resonates with the statement claimed by García and Sylvan (2011) that pupils prefer to draw on their 'diverse language practices for purposes of learning'(p.397), which entails that instructors adopt 'inclusive language practices for the purposes of teaching' (p.397).

On the one hand, Chinese language knowledge is difficult for these students to attain without the help of their preferred and familiar language learning activities in the local educational context. And on the other hand, their Chinese language practices may be rarely facilitated as a result of teachers failing to mobilise and legislate their funds of knowledge formed and retained in the local school-based community. Such students' funds of knowledge tend to take on various shapes, such as their existing, prior, or powerful knowledge accumulated and preserved from their English-speaking language practices, which can be recovered and utilised as their linguistic and cultural capitals for their learning of Chinese in class. Furthermore, connecting a 'funds of knowledge' approach to translanguaging pedagogy supports the dynamic bilingual learners in Chinese class to become involved in such a new languaging environment through utilising and decoding the knowledge that they already know. By doing so, this helps the native teacher-researcher to identify what the students have obtained from the lessons through presenting their Chinese languaging competencies in class. It is suggested that employing their familiar learning activities and favoured instruction styles can more easily engage the local students in the learning content, which can be mutually negotiated and generated among them, thus creating a dialogic learning space in the real Chinese classroom. Here, the local students' Chinese languaging practices and translanguaging capabilities are emerging through employing their various funds of knowledge obtained and sustained in the school-based community. Accordingly, the major forms of students' knowledge are illustrated in the next section, which tend to be shaped and maintained as the funds of knowledge from their formal and informal learning experiences in daily life.

7.3 Prior Knowledge

Being grounded in sociocultural standpoints, 'learning is considered a purely external process,' which 'merely utilises the achievements of development' by virtue of taking in learners' 'previous experience and knowledge' (Vygotsky, 1978, pp.79-80). Based on such a perspective, it is emphasised that language learning is essentially impacted by the students' prior knowledge from their social experiences (Dávila, 2015). In view of that, the teacher's scaffolding strategies become a central point from which the teacher can pinpoint and utilise students' prior knowledge configuration for their further development (Vygotsky, 1978; Dávila, 2015). Modern students are no longer regarded as aimless knowledge followers because:

> They come to formal education with a range of ***prior knowledge, skills, beliefs, and concepts*** that significantly influence what they notice about the environment and how they organize and interpret it. This, in turn, affects their abilities to remember, reason, solve problems, and acquire new knowledge (Bransford, Brown & Cocking, 2000, p.10, italics added).

The local students' prior knowledge (pre-existing knowledge) plays a crucial part in activating their self-initiated and self-sustained potential for receiving fresh information, and thus enhancing their academic achievement (Tobias, 1994; Hailikari, Nevgi & Lindblom-Ylänne, 2007; Roth & Erstad, 2013). Nevertheless, it is contended that a meaningful learning process lies in discovering and making use of the learners' declarative prior knowledge (on 'knowing that')[1], along with their procedural prior knowledge (on 'knowing how')[2] as the two types of knowledge base which contribute to the development of learning trajectories and personal abilities in different dimensions (Hailikari, Katajavuori & Lindblom-Ylänne, 2008).

The category of the local students' pre-existing knowledge should be prioritised for the purpose of better integrating such knowledge into their learning of Chinese at the very initial teaching stage. Accordingly, the Chinese teacher-researcher assumes the main role of recognising and mobilising the linguistic and cultural inventories that students have formed (what they already know) for supporting them to acquire new understandings of Chinese knowledge in a process of being self-directed and employing higher-thinking (how they attain the novel information). Progressively,

1 Prior knowledge is mainly composed of declarative knowledge and procedural knowledge (Dochy, ascited in Hailikari et al., 2008). Declarative prior knowledge belonging to the lowest level is identified as 'the knowledge of facts and meanings that a student is able to remember or reproduce,' being related to 'knowing that' (Hailikari et al., 2008, p.2; Anderson, as cited in Hailikari et al., 2007, p.322).

2 In the meanwhile, procedural prior knowledge is 'characterised by an ability to integrate knowledge and understand relations between concepts and, at the highest level, apply this knowledge to problem-solving,' being referred to as 'knowing how' (Hailikari et al., 2008, p.2; Anderson, as cited in Hailikari et al., 2007, p.322).

the newly-learned knowledge influenced by their prior intellectual capitals has the tendency to be consolidated and upheld, and then turns into their existing knowledge.

7.4 Existing Knowledge

As for the local students' existing knowledge, here it is primarily concerned with the Chinese knowledge that has been shaped and preserved from their previous engagement with learning Chinese in the school-based community. For instance, such existing Chinese knowledge may include some basic Chinese oral expressions, as well as some Chinese writing skills, which can in turn equip them with the advanced expertise for reaching a 'much wider potential range of (Chinese) language and literacy practices' (Duff et al., 2013, p.82). In this regard, exploring inclusive instruction strategies to 'validate their existing knowledge' (p.82) for 'seeking further growth' (p.83) becomes a focus for the Chinese teacher-researcher, instead of ignoring such intellectual treasures along with their educational meanings (Duff et al., 2013).

With the assistance of such existing knowledge, the local students not only tend to increase their exposure to printed and digitised Chinese learning materials on their own, but also broaden their interactions with more Chinese lovers and pursuers in a hybrid learning space. Apart from their existing Chinese knowledge, it is anticipated that other content of their existing knowledge will be further developed into their powerful knowledge for the purpose of fully capitalising on the procedural prior knowledge (regarding 'know how') during the process of bettering their learning of Chinese.

7.5 Powerful Knowledge

Based on the notions of prior knowledge and existing knowledge, powerful knowledge as an alternative form of the students' funds of knowledge has gained more and more attention by developing 'expert students' and deploying their influential 'knowledge structures' (Kinchin, 2016, p.5). The expert student is 'one who recognises the existence and complementary purposes of different knowledge structures, and seeks to integrate them in the application of practice,' thereby gradually developing their sustainable learning appetites and shaping their optimistic attitudes towards obtaining fresh knowledge (Kinchin, 2011, p.187; Rowe, Fitness & Wood, 2015).

In this case, to construct an effective Chinese language curriculum, the teacher-researcher needs to identify local students' various forms of powerful knowledge and apply them to their daily Chinese learning practices. Under such circumstances, the students are provided with enough space to retrieve and benefit from their powerful knowledge in Chinese class.

However, it is argued that incorporating powerful knowledge into the curriculum construction is indispensable in balancing the usable degree of that knowledge, and the learners' in-built knowledge structures, for sustaining safe and active learning, as well as developing 'tolerant' collections of influential disciplinary knowledge rather than 'hostile' ones (Kinchin, 2016). This is echoed in a clarification by Maton (2014) who argued that 'powerful knowledge comprises not one kind of knowledge but rather mastery of how different knowledge is brought together and changed through semantic waving and weaving' (p.182). In such a situation, the potential impacts of the powerful knowledge tend to be manifested within the students' internalised knowledge structures (Kinchin, 2016).

In summary, on the one hand, the responsibility of the Chinese teacher-researcher lies in extracting the local students' differentiated knowledge embodiments from within their acquired knowledge structures. On the other hand, the ultimate goal is to construct an effective, localised, and student-centred Chinese language curriculum. In doing so, the Chinese teacher-researcher needs to have:

> The ability to manage the different types of knowledge in a sequence that matches not just the needs of the subject, but also that of the student, so that the different kinds of disciplinary knowledge are introduced in such a way that the development of expertise is not compromised (Winch, 2013, p.128).

Therefore, focusing on the prior, existing, and powerful knowledge for Chinese curriculum construction provides an alternative way to better know the Australian local school students in terms of their preferences regarding the learning topics and instruction styles. This is not only conducive to enhancing their sense of ownership for the co-produced Chinese learning materials, but also to establishing their positive identity and encouraging their passions for durably active engagement in learning Chinese.

7.6 Conclusion

Chapters 5, 6, and 7 were dedicated to establishing a theoretic-pedagogical framework for theorising a localised and student-centred curriculum construction for enhancing the learnability of the Chinese language within the Australian education system. The starting point of such a process was based on the notion of 'language as a local practice.' This was followed by the elucidation of related concepts, including 'languaging,' 'translanguaging,' 'situated learning,' 'structure and agency,' 'community of practice,' as well as 'funds of knowledge (prior knowledge, existing knowledge, and powerful knowledge),' which were meanwhile linked to the real context of daily Chinese language teaching and learning practices. In this way, such conceptualised thoughts were presented in a logical style, as they related to two primary roles of this research project. One such role is that they work as the pedagogical tool to direct the Chinese teacher-researcher to conduct practical Chinese language teaching in the real classroom. Their other role is to act as the theoretical instrument to inform the process and procedures of data collection and analysis in this research.

CHAPTER 8

What to Teach ? — Generating Localised Chinese Learning Content from Students' Daily Recurring Sociolinguistic Activities

This chapter investigates students' daily recurring sociolinguistic activities in an Australian local public school through a teacher-researcher program entitled the ROSETE Program. It analyses the evidence from classroom teacher participants' perspectives, as well as student participants' preferences in relation to the forms of everyday recurring sociolinguistic activities performed in English during recess at school. Additionally, information from the teacher-researcher's daily observations and teaching experiences in school is also analysed as supplementary evidence. Meanwhile, according to such evidence, a conceptual analysis is provided to explain the concept of making Chinese happen as part of various local practices based on further developing Pennycook's 'language as a local practice' (2010). Following that, the suitable and learnable content sources that were mutually elicited and constructed among the students for their learning of [spoken] Chinese are provided. Then, indigenous Chinese metaphors are adopted to guide the whole process of learning content co-construction and elucidating such evidence conceptually. Based on the conceptual analysis, three conceptualised minds were discovered during the process of knowing the local students to construct learnable and suitable learning content.

8.1 Knowing Local Students' Daily Recurring Sociolinguistic Activities in School-Based Community

The ROSETE Program is a teacher training program that focuses on research orientation and school involvement. The volunteer teacher was allocated to a local public school to conduct Chinese language teaching during the schooldays. As he lacked an Australian Teaching Certificate, one classroom teacher was also required to be present with the Chinese volunteer teacher when he was carrying out the Chinese lessons. Meanwhile, the local classroom teachers were required to monitor the students all day in school, including being on duty for them during recess, as well as playing some sports with them. Therefore, apart from the daily observations and teaching practices in school, it was essential to have an educationally purposeful conversation with these local classroom teachers and students after class, to better know the students' daily recurring sociolinguistic activities as performed in English at school.

This section presents and analyses a variety of students' daily sociolinguistic activities that they frequently performed in English at school. These preferred daily sociolinguistic activities were observed and informed by the classroom teachers and students in this local public school of Western Sydney, and recorded in the teacher-researcher's field notes of daily observations in school. Each of the following subsections is entitled with a theme from the collected evidence.

8.1.1 Gender-Neutral Sports

When it comes to the students' daily recurring sociolinguistic activities in school, there are a variety of popular forms of activities among the students that are frequently performed in English. One of the classroom teachers mentioned four main daily school activities including 'dancing, [doing] lots of sports, rope skipping, as well as singing [songs]' (Classroom Teacher, Ms. Shen, Year 3, 19/06/2017), which would be useful resources for students' learning of [spoken] Chinese. In terms of the sports frequently played at school, Ms. Shen told me that:

> Students like doing lots of sports, like soccer, basketball, as well as every

morning, handball, and skipping, too (Classroom Teacher, Ms. Shen, Year 3, 19/06/2017).

Another classroom teacher emphasised that:

> These role activities, like soccer, volleyball, handball, and table tennis that the kids do in the playground [during recess], and the activities we do in our sports time. These sports are in students' sports sheets (Classroom Teacher, Mr. Ke, Year 4, 20/06/2017).

The popularity of theses ports events in school, including playing handball, basketball and soccer were also expressed by students. They showed great interest in doing these activities at school every day. For instance:

> Students simultaneously repeated their response towards 'handball, handball, handball, handball, handball, handball...' (Focus Group C, Year 5, 19/06/2017).

Students from another group indicated that:

> They were eager to learn topics regarding Chinese basketball, pingpong, and music next term (Focus Group A, Year 3, 19/06/2017).

One of the focus groups also highlighted that:

> They are familiar with the activities, like drawing, playing volleyball and pingpong. Meanwhile, two students from this group — Junwei and Haoran suggested that maybe next term we can do more sports on the grass (Focus Group B, Year 4, 20/06/2017).

Meanwhile, as a Chinese volunteer teacher in school during my schooldays I noticed that:

> In the morning, when I arrived at school and observed the activities they played on the playground, students from one of my Chinese classes ran towards me and said 'nǐhǎo – 你好' (hello) to me. After that, they invited me to join them and showed me how to play bounce ball - handball. By means of this kind of playground activity, I can not only learn something from them, including skills of

> playing bounce ball, but also obtain more opportunities to interact with them in their daily activities (Field Notes, 23/08/2016).
>
> Most students played handball on the playground in the morning and during the recess in this local public school. Meanwhile, I also noticed that almost every student can play handball very well and know the rules of this sport activity in school. Sometimes, students would invite me to play handball with them together, while explaining the basic rules of playing handball to me by using the frequently occurring linguistic terms in this sport (Field Notes, 07/02/2017).

According to these local students' and classroom teachers' feedback, as well as the teacher-researcher's daily observations, gender-inclusive sports, such as playing handball, pingpong, basketball, and soccer, are daily recurring sociolinguistic activities for students in this public school. The fact that these gender-neutral sports are so frequently played suggests that the Chinese words for the terms used in these sports might be effectively employed in teaching Chinese in class. More importantly, handball, pingpong, and basketball are favoured by both male and female gender groups. Meanwhile, these ball sports are compulsory components of local students' sports curriculum during their sporting time in school.

Accordingly, as the four-character Chinese metaphor 'xuéyǐzhìyòng' (学以致用) goes, this teacher-researcher thought of putting what has been learned into practice during the process of learning some abstract knowledge. In this case, handball, pingpong, and basketball are these local students' daily recurring sports activities. Such forms of students' recurring sociolinguistic practices provide them with more access to using [spoken] Chinese during the process of performing these sporting events in the school-based community. Namely, doing these sports-related interactive practices exposes these students to employing the corresponding Chinese linguistic terms for such tangible activities from real life. In that way, students themselves are no longer merely 'sports-related watchers', they benefit from more physical activities, instead of just receiving 'dead' information (Koedinger, Kim, Jia, McLaughlin & Bier, 2015). Consequently, performing the recurring sports events makes the adoption of [spoken] Chinese happen more easily, and with greater frequency. This is not only likely to get them familiar with the intangible Chinese

language in the form of concrete sporting-related practices, but also to enhance opportunities for using Chinese in the local context.

However, when being asked something in relation to a ball game called netball, which was also mentioned by many students in Chinese class, especially among the girls, one of the classroom teachers said:

> Oh, more girls like netball, but if you did netball the boys probably would not like it. Because it seems netball is more the girls' dominant sport, the girls love netball. But the boys, it might be not their favourite if you suggest playing netball. Basketball is probably better. Because when girls play netball, the boys would probably think that, oh, that is the girls' sport (Classroom Teacher, Ms. Li , Year 5, 19/09/2017).

It was clear that many girls preferred to play netball, and that it was the girls' favourite sport in school. Few boys like playing it, because they regard it as a girls' sport. Such a finding is consistent with Taylor's argument (2001) that netball, deriving from original forms of basketball, takes on several resemblances with basketball, which is habitually played more by females than males. Therefore, in terms of outdoor activities, it was advised that basketball would be the better choice, because it is not seen to be so heavily gendered and is more gender-neutral.

8.1.2 Birthday Celebration

The teacher-researcher's observations also focused on another form of daily recurring sociolinguistic activity in school – birthday celebration through singing the English song 'Happy Birthday to You' with the well-known melody, which is always undertaken by the students and their classroom teachers inside the classroom. This was also discussed with various classroom teachers and focus group students through informal professional conversations. The relevant themes that emerged from the conversations are shown as follows. According to Ms. Shen:

> Students have songs in English that they sing, while they are skipping [rope]. For instance, they sing 'teddy bear, teddy bear, turn around.' They really like things with some rhythm (Classroom Teacher, Ms. Shen, Year 3, 19/06/2017).

In addition, when students were asked about their preferred topic concerning learning Chinese, these children raised their voices, saying simultaneously:

> Music, music, Chinese music...! Meanwhile, three boys cannot help expressing their knowledge regarding music. Namely, Tianlei said, 'I know how to play [a] kind of music.' Haoxuan mentioned, 'I know the guitar.' Bowen added, 'I can know any music' (Focus Group A, Year 3, 19/06/2017).

Apart from the above discussions, two simultaneous and unexpected events occurred after the Chinese lessons. This teacher-researcher observed that:

> One day, at the end of a Chinese lesson, one classroom teacher said that today was Meilin's birthday, let us say 'happy birthday' to her. Just at that moment, I encouraged all the other students, and the classroom teacher to say 'shēngrì kuàilè, Měilín.' I noticed that all of them were willing to follow me to give her birthday wishes in Chinese. When I was leaving the classroom, the classroom teacher led the students to sing the song titled 'Happy Birthday to You' in English (Field Notes, 08/08/2017).
>
> The following Tuesday, in another class, a student was having a birthday. So the same celebratory tradition occurred whereby the class sang 'Happy Birthday' to a girl in the class. What has been observed in both classes is the Australian classroom tradition or habit of students, and their classroom teachers, not just saying 'happy birthday,' but also singing that song as a group to their fellow students. This tradition of singing 'Happy Birthday' potentially can occur up to around thirty times a year when the class sings to a peer. Classroom traditions such as this are normalised when a student's birthday happens (Field Notes, 15/08/2017).

Then, when being probed about the frequency and significance of saying 'Happy birthday' and singing the 'Happy Birthday' song in school, Ms. Li remarked that:

> Yeah, we always sing it when we bring in a cake, so we say 'Happy birthday' and sing 'Happy Birthday.' I think that is a good idea. Because that is a song that they already know, so it is easy for them to learn. They have already known the

tune, the background, music. So it is easy for them to catch on to that song and learn that. And something that they can relate to that song as well. So it is not something that, I guess, is foreign to them — make them know the happy birthday song (Classroom Teacher, Ms. Li Year 5, 19/09/2017).

As the above information indicates, the local school students show a great preference for music, and events or activities which are accompanied by unforgettable childhood melodies. In the meantime, there exists a school ritual in Australia which is to celebrate someone's birthday by way of saying 'happy birthday' orally and singing the birthday song 'Happy Birthday to You' during school time. A bold level of confidence in participating in the sung form seems to emerge naturally. Finally, by its very nature of being the international 'birthday song,' students pick up the rhythm quickly, the expression of rhythm being widespread within the local school context, and which is another embodiment of the students' daily recurring sociolinguistic activity at school. Therefore, learning [spoken] Chinese is likely to seem easier not only when the material is familiar to the local school students, but also when it is part of a celebratory practice.

The concept of 'making use of the Chinese language in local celebratory practices' through singing the world-renowned birthday song with its memorable tune in the school-based environment, echoes the notion put forward by Singh, Han, and Ballantyne (2014) that native Chinese volunteer teachers should explore the local students' authentically culturally-related and regularly accessible sociolinguistic activities, for instance, singing with the familiar and attractive rhythms, to make the use of Chinese happen naturally in such specific school-based daily practices. This entails that Chinese teachers of the local school students not can, but should recognise and adopt the students' prior knowledge of the internationally popular birthday song in English, as they already know the tune. Teaching for L1 (English) to L2 (Chinese) transfer would be more effective, because the tune is the same regardless of whether it is sung in English or Chinese.

8.1.3 Mathematical Calculations

The Australian NSW Department of Education is committed to developing students' literacy and numeracy abilities from the very start of their kindergarten assessment through to the end of Year 12. Specifically, on the website of this public school, it was found that:

> NSW's 'Kindergarten Best Start Assessment' is carried out to help parents and teachers identify the children's literacy understandings and numeracy skills before their formal learning in this school (Field Notes, 19/09/2017).

Progressively, various learning programs from the local government education bodies are provided to support students from different stages who encounter learning difficulties in extending their numeracy capabilities in school. For instance:

> Learning programs aimed to cultivate students' accuracy and efficiency in numeracy, such as 'Quick Smart Numeracy' are frequently conducted in the form of pair or individual tutorials in this school (Field Notes, 19/09/2017).

Mathematical calculation activities are fundamental to students' daily school lives, which are also aspects of their recurring sociolinguistic activities at school. When these students were asked what they expected to learn from Chinese lessons, they informed the Chinese teacher-researcher by replying:

> Math...! Can we learn Chinese math? And then Chinese writing — I want to write some Chinese — numbers and Chinese mathematics. Can we do some Chinese mathematics? (Focus Group A, Year 3, 19/06/2017).

As for the mathematical calculations, a classroom teacher mentioned that:

> They do a lot of math in school. I think they will enjoy that (Classroom Teacher, Ms. Li , Year 5, 19/09/2017).

Mathematical calculations are part of these students' daily recurring calculating practices at school. Various teaching instruments and learning modules in relation to instruction in mathematical calculations are performed, especially in the junior classes, at this local public school every day. Such a situation rightly creates a supportive learning space for making the Chinese language relevant to mathematical calculation activities.

Integrating such subjects as mathematics, geography, and science into a language-oriented learning task is conducive to enhancing the students' use of the target language in a learner-focused environment (Bailey, 2015). Correspondingly, through practising such processes, students' learning gains are reciprocally embedded into two facets due to its dual-focused nature, focusing on both content information and language purpose (Mehisto, 2012). To be exact, combining content from other subjects into a language-based learning program can enormously and effectively facilitate learners' metalinguistic perception regarding the intangible language symbols of the corresponding subject field, such as mathematics (Surmont, Struys, van Den Noort & van De Craen, 2016). This would contribute to students' use of [spoken] Chinese during the process of carrying out mathematical practices in the school-based community, especially when the content is closely relevant to these students' daily learning subject — mathematics. More importantly, their high level of participation in the learning of such mathematical content, with regard to those linguistic terms which normally and necessarily occur in making mathematical calculations, will also give rise to them speaking Chinese naturally, and then habitually. Thus, mathematics can become a creative channel for enriching the local students' learning of [spoken] Chinese due to its regularity and importance for both female and male students in school.

8.1.4 Canteen Shopping

Shopping in the canteen is also an indispensable daily activity in this school.

> There is a canteen located in a corner of campus. During recess and lunch time, a lot of students would gather and line up here to buy their favourite food, such as bananas, mandarins, apples, bottled water, spring rolls, Chinese fried rice, and sushi rolls from this school canteen (Field Notes, 19/09/2017).
>
> The food is always sold in the form of a package with a reasonable price tagged as '$5 meal deal' (Field Notes, 19/09/2017).
>
> Furthermore, this local public school is involved in a well-established program in the western suburbs of Sydney, known as 'Crunch & Sip.' Such a program is an easy way to help the kids stay healthy and happy. Meanwhile, it

provides the students, teachers, and staff with an opportunity of eating vegetables and fruit during an allocated Crunch & Sip break during school time (Field Notes, 19/09/2017).

Shopping practice at this canteen is also part of these students' daily recurring sociolinguistic activities in school. To increase the awareness of the importance of eating vegetables and fruit, as well as drinking water at school, this canteen employs the Crunch & Sip program. Namely, it improves students' access to buying healthy food at the school canteen during breaks. Such shopping practice at this school canteen involves the use of various and resourceful English linguistic terms in relation to initiating a shopping conversation; asking for food, exchanging food for money, expressing thanks, as well as ending a shopping conversation. That is to say, this sort of real-life activity can allow these students to use 'live language,' as it would occur in an outside school shopping dialogue, allowing them to transfer such daily concrete practice to potential [Chinese] knowledge attainment (Herrington, Reeves & Oliver, 2014).

8.1.5 Chess

Playing chess is a popular game among local students. In school, it was found that:

> Students not only always play chess in a specifically designed area with the real chess pieces on the playground, but also every year some of them attend a chess competition held by the local Department of Education on behalf of their own school (Field Notes, 20/06/2017).
>
> Meanwhile, in classroom, there are many boxes of chess pieces and chess boards for students to learn how to play chess (Field Notes, 20/06/2017).

Based on the above information, students develop a great interest in chess at school due to their easy access to such equipment, playing it in the playground and the classroom. There are chess tournaments among local students held by the Education Department, intended to cultivate their interest and capabilities in playing chess during school time and after school. It is another opportunity for the students

to use [spoken] Chinese as they play a game, in this case, chess. What is more, a chess game, by its very nature of being 'commonly played according to rules,' with its unique 'frequently used linguistic terms and normally nominated piece roles' allows both genders, without being age- or grade-specific, to participate in it with a certain high frequency within the school setting. Playing chess is another typical example of the local students' everyday recurring sociolinguistic activities in school. Therefore, this daily recurring sociolinguistic activity in school — playing chess, abounds with available content resources for the local students' learning of [spoken] Chinese.

8.2 Eliciting Learnable Chinese Teaching Content from Students' Daily Recurring Sociolinguistic Activities

This particular school is well-provided with sports courts and sporting equipment for students' use during recess and lunch. That is to say, students have easy and convenient access to ball sports during school time. It is a tradition that a student's or teacher's birthday is celebrated with the saying and singing of 'Happy birthday' in class. These and other embodiments of students' daily recurring sociolinguistic activities in school, including making mathematical calculations, shopping at the school canteen, and playing chess, are full of suitable and learnable content, which can be applied to the learning of [spoken] Chinese. Therefore, the following section will focus on how to explore the frequently occurring English linguistic terms in such students' daily recurring sociolinguistic activities undertaken in school.

Evidentiary sources in this section consist of the teacher-researcher's lesson plans, field notes, learning materials for daily Chinese teaching practices, as well as educationally purposeful conversations with the students and their classroom teachers. These evidentiary excerpts were analysed to explore, select, and produce the appropriate and retrievable teaching content for the local students' learning of [spoken] Chinese. In this section, the teacher-researcher describes how he used units of work, or weekly Chinese lesson plans, as the starting point to exemplify the process of generating the localised learning content in class.

8.2.1 Sports Activities-Based Learning Content

In terms of the Chinese teaching content sources from the above-mentioned local students' daily recurring ball sports, such as playing handball, ping pong, and basketball, some instances of learning content generation are illustrated in the following samples of weekly lesson plans. The Chinese teaching plan shown in table 8.1 was to explore the English linguistic terms which occurred in playing handball.

Table 8.1 Chinese lesson plan for exploring linguistic termsoccurring in playing handball

Term 1 & Week 1	**Unit Title: Sports** – shǒuqiú – 手球 **(handball)**	**Date: 21/05/2017**	**Class: Year 3, Year 4 & Year 5**
Expected Learning Outcomes	Initially, the students are expected to be familiar with the meaning and pronunciation of 'shǒuqiú – 手球' (handball). Then, this lesson intends to obtain frequently occurring English linguistic terms in playing handball when a group of students in class show the rules in relation to how to play it in this local school. After learning 'shǒuqiú – 手球' (handball), the students are expected to be able to use this Chinese vocabulary, along with other new expressions when playing handball in the playground.		
Lesson Outline	Review Activity	Reviewing the learned vocabularies used in playing soccer, including 'zúqiú – 足球' (soccer), 'kāiqiú – 开球' (serve the ball), 'chuánqiú – 传球' (pass the ball), 'jiēqiú – 接球' (catch the ball), 'chǎnqiú – 铲球' (tackle) and 'shèmén – 射门' (shoot).	
	Warm-up Activity	Can you teach/show me how to play handball (shǒuqiú – 手球)?	
Teaching Resources & Classroom Arrangement	Equipment to Be Used	The classroom's multimedia equipment, a laser pointer, PowerPoint, a soccer, and a handball.	
	Classroom Arrangement to Be Made	Students will be instructed to stand in a line, and then sit in a circle on the floor when performing the review, and warm-up activities in class.	

As playing handball is a popular sport in this local public school, most students know the rules concerning it. That is to say, they are really knowledgeable when it comes to playing handball. Therefore, after the review activity, a warm-up activity[1] was adopted to elicit the frequently occurring linguistic terms used for playing it. According to the daily observations concerning playing handball, four students are needed to participate. Subsequently, four students were selected in class to act out the real situation of playing handball. The following information was obtained during the process of performing how to play handball. After a quick discussion, it was noticed that the four students separately stood in their own arranged position — 'Kings, Queens, Dance, and Ace.' While they were playing handball, they explained the specific rules. They told me that:

> The King is the first person to start the game by bouncing and passing the ball. Mr. Zhao, you should move to another position when you didn't catch the ball, or to keep the game going. Before you move to another position, you need to dribble the ball (Field Notes, 21/02/2017).

Then, a video about the general rules of playing handball was played. During the process of watching this video, one of the students suddenly raised his hand to inform me that:

> It is a little different from our school's rules of playing handball. At once, the classroom teacher added that the rules you have mentioned are our school's rules. All the students responded with 'yes' simultaneously in class (Field Notes, 21/02/2017).

It was apparent that inviting the students to act out the real situation concerning how to play handball well and properly in this local school, and watching the relevant video, not only made it easy to engage the students in their familiar field and interested topic in Chinese class, but also allowed the teacher-researcher to obtain the four basic verb phrases which frequently occur in playing handball, including 'bounce the ball, pass the ball, catch the ball, and dribble the ball.' It is worth mentioning that

1 It is worth mentioning that such a warm-up activity is adopted as a strategy to elicit the linguistic terms occurring in those students' daily recurring sociolinguistic activities in school, which can be selected and used as the learning content sources for Chinese language teaching. On the one hand, taking ethical issues into consideration, it would help the teacher-researcher to confine the participants to whom he is teaching Chinese. On the other hand, in class it can involve more students' views concerning their topics of interest and preferred content in learning Chinese.

most of the students had mastered how to say 'ball, pass the ball and take the pass' in Chinese from the previous Chinese lessons which concerned soccer. Hence, it was not difficult for them to pronounce and master the above-mentioned frequently used linguistic terms from playing handball. Given the students' learning levels in the Chinese language, the teaching content and learning materials were developed and designed regarding how to play handball in Chinese by using the four frequently occurring verb phrases, namely 'bounce the ball, pass the ball, catch the ball, and dribble the ball.'

With regard to the topic of ping pong, the learning content sources were developed in much the same way as for handball. These students had mastered some basic vocabulary concerning ball sports and their relevant linguistic expressions in Chinese. Therefore, the Chinese lessons for Term 2 from 02/05/2017 to 27/06/2017 were scheduled to make full use of another form of students' daily recurring ball activity — ping pong. The first Chinese lesson of this term began with the following teaching plan. (Table 8.2)

Table 8.2 Chinese lesson plan for exploring linguistic terms occurring in playing ping pong

Term 2 & Week 2	**Unit Title: Sports –** pīngpāngqiú – 乒乓球 **(pingpong)**	**Date: 02/05/2017**	**Class: Year 3 & Year 4**
Expected Learning Outcomes	The teaching purpose for the first Chinese lesson of this term focuses on exploring frequently occurring English linguistic terms in playing ping pong, such as the specified expressions and the necessary equipment in this ball game. After that, the students are expected to be familiar with pronunciations and meanings of such linguistic terms as occur in playing ping pong in Chinese.		
Lesson Outline	Warm-up Activity	Can you say something about ping pong (pīngpāngqiú – 乒乓球) in terms of the following perspectives? A. How to play it (the rules). B. How to calculate/know the scores of two parties. C. What is needed in this sport (sports equipment, people's roles). D. What actions/linguistic terms repeatedly occur in this sport.	

Continued

Term 2 & Week 2	**Unit Title: Sports – pīngpāngqiú – 乒乓球 (pingpong)**	**Date: 02/05/2017**	**Class: Year 3 & Year 4**
Teaching Resources & Classroom Arrangement	Equipment to Be Used	The classroom's multimedia equipment, a laser pointer, PowerPoint, ball(s), bat(s), ping pong table(s) with net(s).	
	Classroom Arrangement to Be Made	Students will be instructed to sit on the floor in the classroom, and then to line up in the area used for playing ping pong in the playground when performing the outdoor learning activity.	

As soon as the discussion question was shown to them, the students actively raised their hands to answer it. They can express their ideas clearly concerning the rules of playing ping pong, the way to calculate the scores of two parties, the equipment needed, as well as the general linguistic expressions frequently occurring in playing ping pong. The students mentioned the necessary equipment used for playing ping pong, including:

> Bat(s), ball, [ping pong] net, and [ping pong] table (Field Notes, 02/05/2017).
>
> Then, I said 'Now please look at this photo attentively (a photograph taken of the ping pong court in school),' adding that 'See, you guys have mentioned all the necessary equipment in English' (Field Notes, 02/05/2017).

In view of the time limitation and schedule for this term, the main learning content focused on the linguistic terms for the ping pong sports equipment which students necessarily and repeatedly use in the course of playing ping pong during recess at school. Other aspects, such as the English expressions for scoring in ping pong, were gradually immersed into this term's Chinese lesson plans during the process of students' learning.

When it came to the topic of basketball, the students demonstrated their great interest and fondness. Thus, the Chinese teaching plan illustrated in Table 8.3 was applied for gathering students' resourceful linguistic repertoire with reference to playing basketball at the beginning of Term 3 in 2017.

Table 8.3 Chinese lesson plan for exploring linguistic terms occurring in playing basketball

Term 3 & Week 1	**Unit Title: Sports – lánqiú – 篮球 (basketball)**	**Date: 08/08/2017**	**Class: Year 3 & Year 5**
Expected Learning Outcomes	Initially, the students are expected to be familiar with the meaning and pronunciation of 'lánqiú – 篮球' (basketball). Meanwhile, this lesson aims to probe into frequently occurring English linguistic terms pertaining to playing basketball at school, such as the action expressions or the sports equipment. After learning the topic of 'lánqiú – 篮球' (basketball), the students are expected to be able to use such Chinese vocabulary when playing basketball at school.		
Lesson Outline	Warm-up Activity	When it comes to playing basketball (lánqiú – 篮球), can you say something about it? A. How to play it (the rules). B. What is needed in this sport (sports equipment, people's roles). D. What actions/languages repeatedly occur/ are used in this sport.	
Teaching Resources & Classroom Arrangement	Equipment to Be Used	The classroom's multimedia equipment, a laser pointer, PowerPoint, a basketball, the basketball court, and the corresponding equipment.	
	Classroom Arrangement to Be Made	Students will be instructed to sit in a line on the floor in the classroom, and then line up on the basketball court in campus when needed to carry out the practical and interactive activity.	

Based on the discussions with the students last term, the Chinese lessons in Term 3 lasting from 08/08/2017 to 26/09/2017, concentrated on the topic regarding basketball. The local students had a good knowledge of playing basketball at school and showed great interest in it. Students tend to play the role of a sports expert and are more willing to share their views and information concerning their preferred activities in their daily school lives with their teachers in class. Hence, a warm-up activity was specially designed to elicit more information which can be used as suitable learning resources for the following Chinese lessons, in accordance with these students' real learning interests and levels. The potential learning content elicited from such educationally purposeful discussion in class is demonstrated as follows:

As for the rules of playing basketball and the way to express the score, one student, Pengfei[1] mentioned the first action word in playing basketball, 'dribble.' The term 'point' was also elicited in class. At the same time, a girl, Ya'nan was selected to write down the form of a final score '6/10' on the whiteboard, which was used as an example of scoring (Field Notes, 08/08/2017).

In terms of the sports equipment used in playing basketball in school, an extremely shy girl — Yajing even raised her hand to answer the question actively. Then, she was invited to present the basic sports equipment used in playing basketball in front of the whole class:

> During this process, each linguistic term in relation to the sports equipment used for playing basketball was recorded, including 'backboard, basketball hoop, basketball court, and basketball' (Field Notes, 08/08/2017).

As for the actions or terms frequently occurring and used in playing basketball:

> 'Dribble the ball' and 'pass the ball' are two linguistic terms which were mentioned most. I then asked the students 'If you want to get one point, what do you need to do?' What I meant was 'tóu lán' (shoot). Following that, Meilin did the action of 'shoot' to give me her response to this question (Field Notes, 08/08/2017).

Based on these discussions, I noticed that even some shy or naughty students were willing to be involved in the interactive learning activity that they were familiar with and interested in. Namely, the students were knowledgeable and could be experts in some specified areas.

Furthermore, noting the significance of the learning content generated by this process, one classroom teacher from Year 4 commented that:

> It is something that they do on a daily basis. So once they are quite familiar

1 The purposes of giving the students real Chinese names are as follows. Initially, it avoids using these students' real English names in order to protect their identities. More importantly, most of the students show great interest in having a Chinese name that can be used in a real situation if someday they travel to China.

with those words, they can use them in class or in the playground. Just in casual, and that makes that language become more automatic for them, more retrievable (Classroom Teacher, Ms. Shi, Year 4, 19/09/2017).

This classroom teacher pointed out that such sports-based activities are regularly played during the students' daily school lives regardless of seasonal changes or gender factors. Clearly, the sporting field can be utilised as a medium for enriching the local students' learning of Chinese in the school-based context. As suggested by Turnnidge, Côté and Hancock (2014), sporting environment, by its very nature, is effective as a tool to engage students to transfer such obtained skills into other educational fields through sports-based involvements and interactions. It is also claimed that sporting-related settings equip students with the sports-specific knowledge, promoting them to apply such expertise to other learning attainments (Whitley, Farrell, Maisonet & Hoffer, 2017). Such situations can trigger students to speak Chinese to their maximum abilities as a natural result of their participation in the local school-based sporting environment.

8.2.2 Celebratory Song-Based Learning Content

The following data are personal observations which contributed to the generation of learning content in regard to how to express 'happy birthday to you' in Chinese, in the form of singing the world-renowned song 'Happy Birthday to You' (zhùnǐ shēngrì kuàilè – 祝你生日快乐). As mentioned in 8.1.2, two unexpected events, the singing of 'Happy birthday' and saying 'happy birthday to you,' occurred in this school's classrooms after Chinese lessons, reminded and inspired the Chinese teacher-researcher to construct a lesson for instructing them to sing that popular birthday song in Chinese, which is illustrated in table 8.4.

Table 8.4 Lesson plan for learning to sing 'Happy Birthday to You' in Chinese

Term 3 & Week 3	**Unit Title: Singing** – Zhùnǐ shēngrì kuàilè – 祝你生日快乐 **(Happy Birthday to You)**	**Date: 22/08/2017**	**Class: Year 3, Year 4 & Year 5**

Continued

<table>
<tr><td>Expected Learning Outcomes</td><td colspan="2">Initially, the students are expected to be familiar with each word's meaning and pronunciation in 'zhù nǐ shēngrì kuàilè – 祝你生日快乐' (Happy Birthday to You).
After that, the students sing 'Happy Birthday to You' in Chinese while a song video with Chinese lyrics is being played in class.
Later on, the students are expected to be able to sing and say 'happy birthday to you' in Chinese when someone's birthday is announced.</td></tr>
<tr><td>Lesson Outline</td><td>Warm-up Activity</td><td>What will you say to your classmates, friends, teachers, or your parents when their birthday comes?
Subsequently, a song video with the Chinese lyrics is to be played in class in order to get them familiar with the Chinese pronunciation of 'happy birthday to you' and easily engaged in the following learning content concerning how to express 'happy birthday to you' in the Chinese way.</td></tr>
<tr><td rowspan="2">Teaching Resources & Classroom Arrangement</td><td>Equipment to Be Used</td><td>The classroom's multimedia equipment, a laser pointer, PowerPoint, a birthday song video with Chinese lyrics.</td></tr>
<tr><td>Classroom Arrangement to Be Made</td><td>Students will be instructed to sit in a line on the floor or stand up when they need to perform the class learning activity.</td></tr>
</table>

Subsequent conversations held with the classroom teachers about the teacher-researcher teaching the lesson 'Let's learn to sing "Happy Birthday to You" ' in Chinese, separately recalled that:

> Because they really enjoy the singing, they are quite engaged. Naturally, they are listening to the content. I think sometimes when the song has that sort of a little catchy [tune] they catch on the words, too. They really enjoy that (Classroom Teacher, Ms. Li, Year 5, 19/09/2017).
>
> I think that is a very good idea. Because again it is drawing on something that they are already familiar with, something they already know. And they already know what the words mean when they are translated. Again they can work it out with their friends. They know what the singing is about when they are singing 'Happy Birthday.' They really enjoy that (Classroom Teacher, Ms. Shen, Year 3, 07/12/2017).

Choosing a mainstream musical song such as 'Happy Birthday to You' as a learning content source for teaching Chinese would encourage students to speak

Chinese with higher frequency if this was a regular celebratory practice for both pupils' and staff's birthdays during school time. Furthermore, this would be beneficial for the local school students' sustainable learning of Chinese from the perspective of ecological language learning, because of their built-up routine and powerful expertise through acting out the recurring celebratory practice at school – singing the birthday song in Chinese (van Lier, 2008).

8.2.3 Mathematical Calculation-Based Learning Content

As mathematical calculating activity involves with the numbers and symbols, the focuses of the following lesson plan (Table 8.5) for Chinese language teaching during Term 4 in 2017 were on the linguistic terms needed during the process of calculating.

Table 8.5 Lesson plan for making mathematical calculations in Chinese

Term 4 & Week 1	**Unit Title: Calculating – jìsuàn – 计算(calculation)**		**Date: 10/10/2017**	**Class: Year 3, Year 4 & Year 5**
Expected Learning Outcomes	1. You are expected to be familiar with the basic calculation symbols such as, ' + , - , ×, ÷, =' in Chinese [Lesson 1 – Lesson 5]; 2. You are going to use the above symbols and the learned Chinese numbers (from 0 to 10) to make mathematical calculations in Chinese based on your knowledge regarding the rules of calculating [Lesson 2 – Lesson 5]; 3. After a period of learning, you will be able to do calculations in Chinese skilfully outside Chinese class or school, in your daily lives, or maybe later in China.			
Lesson Outline	Warm-up Activity	What are the basic calculation symbols in mathematics?		
	Scaffolding Activity	The students are expected to be able to recall the learned Chinese numbers from 0 to 10 with the visual aid of a popular and catchy video concerning counting numbers in Chinese.		
Lesson Outline	Learning Activity	'Turn Around the Calculation Symbols': Initially, the flashcards with the five calculation symbols will be posted on the whiteboard with magnets. Then, students who are willing to be involved in this activity will be invited to turn around one corresponding flashcard each time, while reading the corresponding calculation symbol loudly in Chinese.		

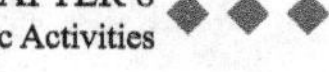

Continued

Term 4 & Week 1	Unit Title: Calculating – jìsuàn – 计算(calculation)	Date: 10/10/2017	Class: Year 3, Year 4 & Year 5
Teaching Resources & Classroom Arrangement	Equipment to Be Used	The classroom's multimedia equipment, a laser pointer, a whiteboard, some magnets, teaching PowerPoint, a video in relation to counting numbers in Chinese, flashcards with the five basic calculation symbols, and the learned Chinese numbers from 0 to 10.	
	Classroom Arrangement to Be Made	Students will be instructed to sit in a line on the floor, and then sit in a circle on the floor or come to the front when conducting the learning activity in class.	

After practicing the established classroom routine in class, the question 'What are the basic calculation symbols in mathematics?' used as the warm-up activity was raised and shown on the screen for students to discuss and involve in learning the Chinese expressions regarding the calculation symbols during Term 4 of 2017.

> A boy, Jiacheng spoke out the basic calculation symbols at one time. I responded that 'Just one is OK once.' Then, Wenjie raised his hand, saying 'Addition.' Yujia mentioned 'Times.' I then proposed a further inquiry on whether it means multiplication. She responded 'Yes.' 'Subtraction' was the following calculation symbol which was pointed out. I continued asking 'Anything else?' Mingxuan looked at me, replying 'Divide by.' Immediately, Junzhe added that 'it is division.' Simultaneously, other students raised their voices, saying 'Me, me, me.' ... As for the last calculation symbol, 'equals' was dug out by a girl, Manni in class. After that, I announced 'Now, I think we have found out the basic calculation symbols, let's look at the screen and check them together' (Field Notes, 10/10/2017).

Combining content with language learning gives rise to some eminent features and advantages. For instance, in the school-based setting, the content-and-language-integrated learning — a pedagogical choice which is both a medium and a catalyst — significantly boosts the beginning learners' confidence and autonomy in accessing the target language through enabling them to engage in real situation-based fruitful learning, thereby maintaining their ongoing learning interest (Coyle, 2013). Using mathematical calculations to learn Chinese linguistic terms which frequently occur in mathematics would reduce the students' unfamiliarity with the learning of Chinese in such an English-dominant circumstance. The process of calculation practice can mobilise their different intellectual modes, namely listening, thinking, speaking, writing, as well as reading. Also, linking mathematical calculations to the learning of [spoken] Chinese would build on these students' existing knowledge concerning making mathematical calculations in English, as well as teaching them to count the numbers in Chinese from 0 to 10. Such knowledge storage is beneficial for students in developing new knowledge regarding the Chinese linguistic terms used for conducting fundamental mathematical calculations.

8.2.4 Canteen Shopping-Based Learning Content

The Chinese lesson plan (in Table 8.6) was designed to discover the linguistic terms frequently used while students were shopping at the school canteen.

Table 8.6 Lesson plan for discovering shopping and popular food language at the school canteen

Term 4 & Week 3	**Unit Title: School Canteen Shopping – gòuwù – 购物 (shopping)**	**Date: 24/10/2017**	**Class: Year 3, Year 4 & Year 5**
Expected Teaching Purposes	To explore the linguistic terms students frequently use while they are shopping at the school canteen, as well as their favourite food on the canteen menu.		
Lesson Outline	Warm-up Activity	Let's act out the real situation when you are shopping at the school canteen. A menu from the school canteen in 2017 is used for your reference about the food you would like to buy.	
	Shopping Language at School Canteen		
	Popular Food at School Canteen		
Teaching Resources & Classroom Arrangement	Equipment to Be Used Classroom Arrangement to Be Made	The classroom's multimedia equipment, a laser pointer, teaching PowerPoint, the latest menu for the school canteen, an apron, some artificial paper money, and paper-made food. Students will be instructed to sit in a line on the floor, and then sit in a circle on the floor or come to the front when conducting the above-mentioned warm-up activity in class.	

In terms of the process of achieving such teaching purposes and obtaining the relevant learning content, the warm-up activity adopted as a strategy was to help the students easily engage in the class learning activity and to elicit more useful information for their subsequent learning of Chinese. It was an activity in which some students acted out the real situation when shopping at the school canteen. A menu of the school canteen in 2017 was prepared for their reference about the food that they would like to buy. Meanwhile, an apron, some artificial paper money, and paper-made food were provided for their performance. Each time, one boy and one girl were chosen to act as a 'sales boy' or a 'sales girl' wearing an apron, as well as holding the menu in his/her hands. Naturally, the other person became a 'buyer.' When hearing 'action' from other peers, they were ready to perform. The following group 'drama performance' left me with a deep impression of the language and vocabulary used for their real shopping experiences at the school canteen. For instance:

> Initially, the boy, Junwei took the initiative to have a conversation with the sales girl — Meijing. He asked 'Can I have a cheese bacon roll?' Subsequently, Meijing responded to him with 'Sure, that would be 10 dollars.' After a while, Meijing added 'Here is your cheese bacon roll.' As a response, Junwei said 'Thanks' to her (Field Notes, 24/10/2017).

Another group's acting was conducted by using a different language style:

> As for this group, the sales boy — Tianyou first asked the buyer — Yuxun'What would you like today?' Then, Yuxun answered 'I would like un... cheese pizza un... and Chinese fried rice.' At once, she asked the sales boy 'How much are they?' After thinking (quickly calculating in his brain) for a while, Tianyou told her 'Ah, 7 dollars and 30 cents.' The conversation for shopping between them went on with the buyer saying 'OK. Here you are,' as well as the sales person responding 'Thank you.' It ended with a basic courtesy expression 'Bye-bye' from the buyer (Field Notes, 24/10/2017).

Meanwhile, in terms of the popular food at the school canteen:

Meat Pie, Sushi Rolls, as well as Chinese Fried Rice are the top three foods among them, discovered through a heated discussion between the students and the Chinese teacher in class (Field Notes, 24/10/2017).

Based on the above-mentioned class discussions, the discovered linguistic repertoires from these students' daily recurring shopping practices in school would be utilised as the learning content sources for the subsequent Chinese lessons. Curriculum construction is based on the students' real-life social practices, especially in language learning classrooms where they are entitled to have their own real voices concerning the selection of learning topics and activities which are meaningful in their daily lives (McKay, 2013). Therefore, selecting the linguistic terms which frequently occur in the students' shopping activity at the school canteen as content sources for teaching Chinese would make it more likely that they would speak in Chinese naturally and regularly in their daily shopping practice. Importantly, teaching Chinese via the authenticity-oriented shopping situation constructs a real and vivid atmosphere for their learning of [spoken] Chinese in the school-based community.

8.2.5 Chess Gaming-Based Learning Content

The Chinese teaching plan illustrated in Table 8.7 was designed to probe into the linguistic terms which frequently occur in playing chess, which can be suitably applied to the local students' learning of Chinese.

Table 8.7 Lesson plan for probing into the linguistic terms occurring in playing chess

Term 3 & Week 2	**Unit Title: Playing Chess – xiàngqí – 象棋(chess)**	**Date: 08/08/2017**	**Class: Year 3 &Year 4**
Expected Teaching Purposes	It will elicit more linguistic terms which occur in playing chess at school, which can be used as suitable learning resources for subsequent Chinese lessons.		
Lesson Outline	Warm-up Activity	When it comes to playing chess at school, can you say something about it? Such as: A. How to play it (the rules). B. What is needed in this game (e.g. equipment). C. What actions/linguistic terms repeatedly occur/are used in this activity.	

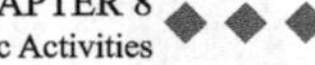

Continued

Term 3 & Week 2	Unit Title: Playing Chess – xiàngqí – 象棋(chess)	Date: 08/08/2017	Class: Year 3 &Year 4
Teaching Resources & Classroom Arrangement	Equipment to Be Used Classroom Arrangement to Be Made	The classroom's multimedia equipment, a laser pointer, teaching PowerPoint, a box of chess pieces. Students will be instructed to sit in a line on the floor, and then sit in a circle on the floor when conducting the above-mentioned warm-up activity in class.	

According to the students' existing chess knowledge and discussions, the following linguistic terms in relation to playing chess were elicited in class:

> In terms of the roles of different chess pieces, they are named as 'Pawn, Castle/Rook, Queen, King, Knight, and Bishop' separately by students at school. After that, students themselves were asked to type each linguistic term on the corresponding chess piece that was presented on the PowerPoint (Field Notes, 08/08/2017).
>
> Two verbs that describe the actions occurring in the process of playing chess, namely 'hold and move' were obtained from the class discussion as well (Field Notes, 08/08/2017).

Connecting game-based enrichment activities with educational purposes into learning content is crucial in capitalising on the students' game-related knowledge, such as team games and board games for accommodating the requirement of curriculum placement at the very initial stage of schooling (Schifter, 2013). Also, in real-life-related situations, game-based immersion education can improve the learners' degrees of self-effort and their corresponding participation, thereby minimising any sense of restlessness in mastering new languages (Cheng, She & Annetta, 2015). Therefore, such 'discovered' linguistic expressions, particularly created and utilised for the purpose of playing a chess game, are of worth as potentially learnable content sources for the local students' learning of [spoken] Chinese.

As the metaphor 'hǎo de kāishǐ shì chénggōng de yībàn – 好的开始是成功的一半' (well begun, half done) goes, knowing the target learners' (the Australian students) characteristics well in the local context, especially in the local school-based environment is a good beginning for Chinese language teaching. Based on the findings from the teacher-researcher's day-to-day teaching practices, the local students showed great initiative in mutually negotiating and constructing the content for their learning of Chinese in class, whereby they helped establish a learning space, enabling them freely to express what they already knew from their daily recurring sociolinguistic activities in the school-based community. By empowering the local students to have discourse power in selecting their preferred and suitable Chinese learning topics and content from their familiar and favoured sociolinguistic activities in school, the knowledge base for the subsequent Chinese lessons tends to be developed and formed from the perspective of being learner-focused, instead of being teacher-centred. According to Singh and Han (2014):

> 'Teaching Chinese with Australian characteristics' embraces a learner-centred approach to the methods and content for making Chinese learnable. This means the teacher-researchers learn to take responsibility for the students' actual learning of Chinese. To do so they generate content for the teaching/learning of Chinese from learners' recurring everyday sociolinguistic activities performed in English, and thus build on their existing sociolinguistic knowledge. They teach forms of Chinese learners can use in everyday lives (pp.418-419).

Being a Chinese teacher-researcher, it is essential to have a better understanding of the Australian local school students' linguistic and cultural repertoires that they bring to the classroom, in order to make Chinese a learnable language within their sociolinguistic contexts (AITSL, 2012). Given the above-mentioned, knowing the local students' linguistic repertoires from their daily recurring sociolinguistic activities at school can help make their hidden knowledge in certain areas transparent, rather than 'buried treasures.' This type of information not only helps the teacher-researcher to identify the local students' preferred and engaged Chinese learning content at the very beginning, but also contributes to making the lesson plans more focused on the students' real interests and learnability during the process of Chinese language teaching.

More importantly, the design of Chinese lesson plans tends to be transferred from being teacher-centred to student-centred, through incorporating more students' views and knowledge into the selection of learning content sources and teaching materials. From this perspective, the students themselves play an important role in selecting their engaged and learnable content. In such a process, the teacher-researcher works more as a facilitator for encouraging the students to retrieve their existing knowledge from their daily recurring sociolinguistic activities in school, which can then be used for their learning of Chinese. Hence, the student-centred pedagogy, as a tour guide, leads the Chinese teacher-researcher to have a better understanding of the local school students, including their interests, knowledge configuration, and potential in learning Chinese.

All in all, the local students are the 'ultimate consumers' of the learning content generated from their daily recurring sociolinguistic activities in school. To evaluate the learnability of such content, it is necessary to take the students' views into account, some of which are presented as follows:

> It was enjoyable because we got to play stuff. I think it is an interesting learning how we can keep basketball, and the game going in Chinese (Focus Group C, Year 5, 19/06/2017).
>
> Now, Chinese learning is enjoyable and fun. I think it is really good we do like Chinese but Chinese is remote from us, now we could use Chinese and we could understand Chinese (Focus Group B, Year 4, 20/06/2017).

Students themselves are the direct and ultimate 'purchasers' of this learning content and the materials produced from their daily recurring sociolinguistic activities. That is to say, students have dual identities in regard to being involved in selecting what to 'buy,' and then how to use such 'products' in their daily lives. This can be compared to the Chinese metaphor 'liàngtǐcáiyī' (量体裁衣)[1]. In this situation, students are not just the 'consumers' who have the power to decide on their suitable stuff — the Chinese learning content, but also have their own preferred

1 The original source of the Chinese version: "卧闲草堂本《儒林外史 》评：非子长之才长于写秦汉；短于写三代；正是其量体裁衣；相题立格；有不得不如此者耳 "。原指按照身材裁剪衣服。比喻按照实际情况办事。Originally, it refers to tailoring according to a person's actual figure or height. Metaphorically, it means that carrying something out should be based on actual circumstances.

way to utilise that stuff in their local context after 'purchasing,' such as doing ball sports, singing celebratory rhythms, making mathematical calculations, shopping at the school canteen and playing chess. In this way, the Chinese teacher-researcher as the 'tailor' would supply the 'customised product' — the suitable learning content which fits the 'clients' — the local students, to a large extent. This can contribute to the information transmission (students' views on their preferred Chinese learning topics and content) between the Chinese teacher-researcher and the local students from the perspective of the crucial clients' (students') feedback concerning the learnability and accessibility of such teaching content for their learning of Chinese.

On the contrary, compared with the student-centered pedagogy the selected learning content from the teacher-centered model may lead to the ultimate consumers' (the local school students') dissatisfaction due to a perceived lack of catering to their real interests and daily access. Therefore, the concept of 'liàngtǐcáiyī' (量体裁衣) directs the Chinese teacher-researcher to concentrate on these 'clients' (the local students) concrete needs to 'tailor' such localised products (Chinese learning content) through using the forms of their favoured daily practices at school, namely the Chinese learning content which is closely connected with these local students' daily uses.

Meanwhile, according to three classroom teachers' comments on utilising such content for their students' learning of Chinese, it has the following features and benefits:

> I think it is good. I think they responded well to it. It is something that they are interested in. It is something that is not too abstract (Classroom Teacher, Ms. Shen, Year 3, 19/06/2017).
>
> I think you have done a great job of selecting concepts or ideas that are important to the students. I think that they could connect with these. And I think that give[s] their real enthusiasm and purpose to learn the words, because they like playing handball, table tennis, and chess. It is really good how you try to connect the type of activities and the things that they do (Classroom Teacher, Ms. Shi, Year 4, 19/09/2017).
>
> You have the photos from the basketball court, you have the photos from the

handball court. So everything you do relates to the space and environment. When Chinese [concepts are] so abstract to them at home, you know, so it attaches them to the Australian culture (Classroom Teacher, Ms. Mu, Year 5, 21/11/2017).

It is clear that this learning content and these materials derive from the local students' sociolinguistic activities, frequently performed in English at school, which are so closely associated with their daily lives. Such resources contribute to generating the teaching content for the students' learning of Chinese, which is reflected in a Chinese metaphor 'jiùdìqǔcái' (就地取材)[1].'jiùdì' (就地) means being closely connected to the local area. 'qǔcái' (取材) refers to obtaining materials and resources. Thus, 'jiùdìqǔcái' (就地取材) is defined as obtaining materials from the local area to make full use of the potential potency of local resources. As is shown in the above-mentioned Chinese teaching plans, the learning units range from popular sporting events, birthday celebratory habits, calculating exercises, school canteen shopping to chess, which cover many of the students' daily recurring sociolinguistic activities in this Australian local primary school. Accordingly, corresponding linguistic terms are elicited from such sociolinguistic activities, as well as those which are selected and utilised as the learning content and materials during the following Chinese teaching practices, to judge whether they are suitable or learnable for the local students' learning of Chinese. Specifically, 'jiùdìqǔcái' (就地取材) at this point informs the Chinese teacher-researcher of the value in exploring the learning content sources and teaching materials based on the Australian local students' recurring sociolinguistic activities from their daily school lives. Such local resources can make Chinese language learning closely connected to their everyday practices at school through activating its prospective effectiveness. That is to say, the above-illustrated learning resources, including the sports-related equipment, the well-known tunes and lyrics of the birthday song, the authentic canteen menu, the mathematics-based instructional tutorials, and chess instruments from the designed lesson plans are based on materials existing in this local public school that are touchable, perceptible,

1 The original source of Chinese version: "噫，岂其娶妻必齐之姜，就地取材，但不失立言之大意而已矣 "。原指就在原地选取材料，用来比喻不依靠外力，充分发挥本身的潜力。(清·李渔《笠翁偶集·三·手足》) It is defined as obtaining materials from the local area to make full use of the potential potency of local resources.

and accessible, which they can experience during their schooling. All these handy elements, with the purpose of educational utilisation, would contribute to making [spoken] Chinese happen naturally and regularly in the real environment of the local school-based community. Guillot (1996) proposed that:

> Exposure to, and familiarity with authentic texts also helps instil confidence in the face of the target language, an important factor in autonomous language learning, as well as spurring learners towards authentic sources. Authentic sources, in turn, tend to stimulate learners to further independent discovery and learning (p.152).

Therefore, it is emphasised that the local students' learning of Chinese can benefit from being exposed to the learning content in relation to such real-life activities, as are regularly performed in English during their school time. The students naturally are able to apply such Chinese expressions, as they play their favourite sports activities, sing the celebratory song, make mathematical calculations, buy food, and play chess in the school-based community. In doing so, it encourages the speaking of Chinese to happen intrinsically among the local students while they are performing various forms of their preferred activities at school.

When it comes to the process of selecting and generating these Chinese learning topics, as well as content, one classroom teacher compared the learning content generated from these students' daily recurring sociolinguistic activities to the main teaching content that a previous Chinese volunteer teacher had adopted in class. He recalled and remarked that:

> They really enjoyed it, particularly [since] you are focusing on a lot of sports and activities this year and last year as well, which was different from what the previous Chinese teacher [did]. And you can tell that the kids really responded very well towards it. While the previous teaching had been focused on the colours, so the days and weeks they feel like [that is just] normal school to them. Because you asked the kids 'What would you like to learn about?' And you often do that with them, they really like that (Classroom Teacher, Mr. Ke, Year 4, 20/06/2017).
>
> I think it really helps them feel a sense of ownership and they really want

> to take that on, because these things they can use every day. And it is not used directing 'We are doing these, we are doing those.' You gave them the choices [as to what they could do], which really again gives them a sense of ownership. They are really communicating in those lessons, because it is the things they really enjoy doing and they engage in [them] very strongly (Classroom Teacher, Mr. Ke, Year 4, 28/11/2017).

This classroom teacher's feedback suggests that the students now have more discourse power to choose their own desired topics in relation to learning Chinese in terms of teaching content and interactive activities through mutual negotiation and construction in class. This classroom teacher's point of view also proposes that when the students' self-determination is given full attention concerning deciding on their desired knowledge creation and intake, for example, their preferred sports-related learning topics and content through working as the co-constructor, their immediate response in class and enduring learning enthusiasm after class, both demonstrate that they are well-involved and show positive attitudes (Swain, 2006). Being supported to create opportunities for voicing themselves, the students are disposed to reshape their roles in learning Chinese, positioning themselves in a democratic learning community whereby they have the right to make well-informed choices on the formation of their preferred learning content. The Chinese language classroom, by its very nature, is a particularly micro-social context in which these local students are entitled to enact their agency through dialoguing interactively, thereby equalising their learning opportunities in such a cooperative environment (Stromquist, 2015; Rigby, Woulfin & März, 2016). It has been suggested that students' sense of self-agency would help to develop a sympathetic and participative classroom atmosphere, which is built through the process of dialogical communication in class, rather than a competitive and disengaged one (Clarke, Howley, Resnick & Rosé, 2016).

More importantly, these students' expectations towards such learning content and preferred activities in Chinese lessons were fulfilled to a certain extent. That is to say, they were not just given the freedom to co-construct their anticipated Chinese language knowledge, but also experienced a learning process during which that jointly generated content was taught and retained in a creative and enjoyable way.

Since students are the 'ultimate consumers' of such learning content, being active mediators in discovering their expected learning content would help them form the 'zhǔrénwēng yìshí – 主人翁意识' (a sense of ownership/belonging) in learning Chinese through empowering, instead of restraining their capabilities to take actions. By doing so, these students' agencies can be mobilised and deployed to help them achieve the anticipated learning outcomes under a negotiable and harmonious learning space (Swain, 2006; Rigby, Woulfin & März, 2016).

8.3 Encounters of 'liàngtǐcáiyī' (量体裁衣), 'jiùdìqǔcái' (就地取材) and 'zhǔrénwēng yìshí' (主人翁意识) in the process of generating the localised learning content

This section starts with providing a conceptual link that features the forms of the local students' daily recurring sociolinguistic activities, as performed in English at school, through the process of discovering the students' anticipated learning topics and content.

Local students' daily recurring sociolinguistic activities in school include playing gender-neutral sports, singing catchy rhythms, making mathematical calculations, shopping at the school canteen, as well as playing chess. Such regularly occurring sociolinguistic activities performed in English constitute five daily practices among these students within this school-based community.

The concept of 'language as a local practice' (Pennycook, 2010) deals with three aspects concerning how language works as a series of activities within a certain space and place. Namely, taking into consideration 'language,' 'locality,' and 'practice' as the three constituents and investigating the mechanism between them informs us that language arises from the events which it enables. That makes language an embodiment of social and spatial activities in people's daily lives, instead of an intangible object (Lankiewicz, 2014). Any one language is the creation of socially situated happenings, and is part of the action (Karrebæk, Madsen & Møller, 2015). Grounded in the above-mentioned concepts and analysed evidence, [spoken] Chinese happens in these sporting practices, celebrating practice, calculating practice, shopping practice, and chess games in the local school context. Such daily recurring practices in school allow the local school students to express their original ideas concerning the selection and construction of suitable and learnable teaching content for their learning of [spoken] Chinese.

However, according to the Australian K-10 syllabus for the Chinese language, there exists one phenomenon which is the one-size-fits-all stereotype in terms of the selection of learning content. For instance, to cultivate the local students' ability concerning spoken Chinese, the syllabus claims that students should learn to engage in conversations with such sentence patterns as 'Qǐng wèn …?' (BOSTES, 2003, p.30), while it is actually a very typical sentence pattern used in a formal conversation between teacher and student to express some requests in a polite way in China. Meanwhile, its main aim is to develop the Australian students' communication skills by 'focusing on languages as systems' (BOSTES, 2003, p.13), rather than focusing on 'language as a local practice.' In this regard, the reference document is essentially designated for constructing the Chinese curriculum, looking at Chinese language learning as a static entity rather than a dynamic and interactive process, and in doing so fails to marry it to the local school-based authentic context (Jørgensen, 2008). Such a stance and focus neglects the essence and importance of the actual uses of learning Chinese (the process for languaging Chinese) in real-world situations (Jørgensen, 2008; Pennycook, 2010; García & Wei, 2014). This also means over-emphasising the grammatical features and correctness of the target language — Chinese, which can impair the local beginning learners' interest and confidence in learning it. It is thus very difficult to achieve such a goal by using learning content which is far removed from the students' daily lives, or without any help from contextual factors.

Furthermore, as to the learning outcomes (e.g. for Stage 2), it is required that a student should 'recognise and respond to spoken texts in familiar contexts' (BOSTES, 2003, p.15). This also poses some unasked questions, including that of what the familiar contexts to students mean here, and how can the familiar contexts be created. That is to say, the existing Australian K-10 syllabus is inadequate for meeting 'the needs and objectives of how L1 English speakers learn Chinese' in the local school context (Zhang & Li, 2010, p.92). Rather, employing a 'liàngtǐcáiyī'(量体

裁衣) concept would adapt Chinese language learning content to the Australian local practices. Such topics and content mutually negotiated and constructed by the local school students in Chinese class would be selected as a 'customised model' to cater to their real interests and needs in terms of learning Chinese with Australian characteristics (Singh & Han, 2014). That entails the production of an inventory of Chinese learning content from 'a set of bundled activities that are repeated over time' (Pennycook, 2010, p.3), which is 'embedded in the learners' locality and embodied in their everyday sociolinguistic activities' (Singh & Han, 2014, p.415).

To make [spoken] Chinese a daily practice of Australian school students in this case study, the co-construction of potentially learnable content between the Chinese teacher-researcher and the local school students must be considered. If the Chinese teacher-researcher ignores the local school students' intellectual dominance and their linguistic repertoires, then such 'valuable resources' would be simply overlooked during the process of generating suitable Chinese learning content.

During the process of knowing the local students' daily recurring sociolinguistic activities in school, adopting the Chinese concepts of 'liàngtǐcáiyī' (量体裁衣), 'jiùdìqǔcái' (就地取材), and 'zhǔrénwēng yìshí' (主人翁意识) creates opportunities for localising such learning content for Chinese language teaching based on mutual negotiation, selection, and construction. Here, employing 'liàngtǐcáiyī' (量体裁衣), 'jiùdìqǔcái' (就地取材), and 'zhǔrénwēng yìshí' (主人翁意识) helps the Chinese teacher-researcher to identify Australian students' recurring sociolinguistic activities in school, which can encourage students to use [spoken] Chinese in their daily practices within the local environment. This would extend what Pennycook (2010) has proposed, that ' "language as a local practice" is not only repeated social activity involving language, but is also, through its relocalisation in space and time, a process of change' (p.137). Pennycook (2010) elucidates that 'language, locality, and practice' (p.137) — the three constituents make up 'language as a local practice.' The relationship between language, locality, and practice is relevant in localising Chinese that draws on such students' daily social practices in school, reflecting their local characteristics, to meet their interests and needs in learning [spoken] Chinese (Pennycook, 2010; Singh & Nguyễn, 2018). Meanwhile, the local school students are the 'ultimate consumers' of such Chinese learning content. Therefore, the role of the Chinese metaphors, namely 'liàngtǐcáiyī' (量体裁衣), 'jiùdìqǔcái' (就地取材), and 'zhǔrénwēng yìshí' (主人翁意识) working as the 'tour guide' leads the teacher-researcher to construct the localised, learnable, and appropriate Chinese learning content for the local school students.

The proposition is to make [spoken] Chinese an embodiment of local practices. This requires 'digging out' diverse forms of daily practices from local students' school lives, which can help make [spoken] Chinese part of such practices through utilising the localised learning content. Such a proposition is reinforced by language, locality, and practice as a means of permeating our awareness of how the Chinese language functions as a united social and spatial practice, in view of the shift from language to 'languaging' for second/foreign language education (Jørgensen, 2008; Pennycook, 2010; Leeman, 2012). Put another way, such Chinese concepts as 'liàngtǐcáiyī' (量体裁衣), 'jiùdìqǔcái' (就地取材), and 'zhǔrénwēng yìshí' (主人翁意识) presuppose that the local students' agency is activated to have an equal discourse power in the co-construction of localised learning content based on their daily recurrent social practices within a negotiable structure in the Chinese classroom. Accordingly, the function of such daily recurring sociolinguistic activities among these students is to make [spoken] Chinese occur naturally as part of the local sporting, celebrating, calculating, shopping and gaming practices, which 'takes us away from abstract systems and competencies and focuses instead on language as a social activity' (Pennycook, 2010, p.124). In fulfilling such a presupposition, apart from generating localised Chinese learning content, the corresponding teaching strategies adopted also play an important part, which will be presented and discussed in the following section.

8.4 Conclusion

This section explored the forms of the local students' daily recurring sociolinguistic activities, as performed in English at school. The analysis section revealed that the five basic students' daily practices that regularly occurred in this local public school included playing sports, celebrating birthdays, calculating numbers, purchasing food, as well as playing chess. Subsequently, this section further explained the potentially learnable and appropriate content for these local students' learning of [spoken] Chinese through mutual negotiation and construction between the teacher-researcher and the students in class. Accordingly, it is proposed that it is possible to set the conditions to encourage the speaking of Chinese to happen regularly and naturally as part of such local practices, based on Pennycook's statement (2010) 'language as a local practice.' Following such a notion, during the process of knowing the local school students' daily recurring sociolinguistic activities, three Chinese metaphors are adopted, including 'liàngtǐcáiyī' (量体裁衣), 'jiùdìqǔcái' (就地取材) and 'zhǔrénwēng yìshí' (主人翁意识) for guiding the teacher-researcher to generate the localised Chinese teaching content for their learning and use of [spoken] Chinese in the local context.

The students' in-class engagement after utilising such localised learning content, and utilising their preferred instruction styles in mastering Chinese will be the focus of analysis in the next evidentiary section. Evidence of this engagement will take the form of the teacher-researcher's field notes from weekly Chinese teaching practices in class, as well as the classroom teachers' and the students' views and feedback after class.

CHAPTER 9

How to Teach ? — Utilizing Multidimensional Student-Centered Instruction Strategies to Mobilise Students' Funds of Knowledge

Chapter 8 explored the forms of students' daily recurring sociolinguistic activities in the school-based community within the context of an Australian local public school. Based on such students' daily practices in school, the potential content sources that would be suitable for their learning of Chinese were identified by mutual discussion, selection, and construction in class. The process of how to subsequently utilise such teaching content to make Chinese learnable for them is presented in this section. The analysis of the relevant lesson plans and field notes, as well as the students' and their classroom teachers' comments, facilitated the Chinese teacher-researcher to identify learning activities and teaching strategies that can provide the local students with optimum opportunities for making the content learnable for them. This further provided the teacher-researcher with another route to acquiring a better understanding of the local students in terms of their learning habits and styles. This analysis aims to ascertain how such learning content and teaching strategies can jointly reveal, retrieve, and re-use the local students' diverse forms of funds of knowledge in the school-based community to make Chinese learnable.

Therefore, the following section addresses how the Chinese teacher-researcher used the content generated from the above-mentioned students' daily recurring sociolinguistic activities to conduct regular Chinese language teaching by creating the relevant lesson plans, and considering his field notes, as well as the standpoints and responses informed by the students and their classroom teachers.

9.1 Xǐwénlèjiàn – 喜闻乐见[1] activities

Various learning activities and teaching strategies were performed and practised through the integration of the content derived from students' daily recurring sociolinguistic activities at school. The following themes were derived from information sources, such as the teacher-researcher's daily teaching plans and field notes, as well as the students' feedback and their classroom teachers' comments, which are to be discussed collectively as the units of analysis.

9.1.1 Teaching Linguistic Terms Identified from Playing Handball

The lesson plan in Table 9.1 demonstrates the teaching practices in relation to the process of learning the linguistic terms which were identified in playing handball.

Table 9.1 Chinese lesson plan for teaching linguistic terms used in playing handball

Term 1 & Week 3—Week 10		**Unit Title: Sports – shǒuqiú – 手球 (handball)**	**Date: 14/02/2017—04/04/2017**	**Class: Year 3, Year 4 & Year 5**
Expected Learning Outcomes	Speaking (Pronunciation) Listening (Responding) Familiarity (Daily Usage)	Initially, this lesson is to make students familiar with the meanings and pronunciations of the following four verb phrases which occurred frequently in the playing of 'shǒuqiú – 手球,' including, 'pāiqiú – 拍球' (bounce the ball), 'chuánqiú – 传球' (pass the ball), 'jiēqiú – 接球' (catch the ball) and 'dàiqiú – 带球' (dribble the ball) through conducting an interactive activity entitled 'Minion Says.'		

1 The original source of Chinese version: 明·王守仁《王文成公全书》:"仆诚喜闻而乐道，自顾何德以承之。" It originally means what one really loves to hear and see, which is extremely popular among people.

Continued

<table>
<tr><th colspan="2">Term 1 & Week 3—Week 10</th><th>Unit Title: Sports – shǒuqiú – 手球 (handball)</th><th>Date: 14/02/2017—04/04/2017</th><th>Class: Year 3, Year 4 & Year 5</th></tr>
<tr><td>Expected Learning Outcomes</td><td>Speaking (Pronunciation)
Listening (Responding)
Familiarity (Daily Usage)</td><td colspan="3">Subsequently, employing a game entitled 'Charades' helps them enhance their memorisation of the learned Chinese vocabulary and verb phrases concerning playing handball from the perspective of pronunciations and meanings.
Finally, 'a Drawing/Designing Activity' will be used as an evaluation activity to let the students present their learning outcomes in class.
After learning these four commonly used verb phrases in this game, it is hoped that the students will use these Chinese vocabulary when playing handball in the school playground.</td></tr>
<tr><td>Lesson Outline</td><td>Class Learning Activities</td><td colspan="3">Minion Says:
In class, when a question is posed, such as 'Who can remember what we have learnt from the last Chinese lesson and how to say ... in Chinese' by acting out 'Minion Says.'
A Game: Charades
1. Work in pairs.
2. One student uses his/her language and action to describe the word given, but he/she cannot give any clues about the pronunciation or spelling of that word.
3. The other student needs to speak out that word in Chinese very quickly.
4. After two words are finished, the two students swap roles.
Note: the less time you use, the more chances you have to be the winner.</td></tr>
<tr><td rowspan="2">Lesson Outline</td><td>Class Evaluation Activity</td><td colspan="3">A Drawing/Designing Activity:
1. Three students work in a group;
2. Draw/design a real situation for playing shǒuqiú (手球) as you always do in the playground such as: four players are needed; their different positions/roles; the actions used in playing shǒuqiú (手球).</td></tr>
<tr><td>Teacher's Role</td><td colspan="3">The teacher's role will be as an instructor and a facilitator during the process of giving a lecture and conducting the class activities separately.</td></tr>
</table>

Afterwards, these students' in-class involvement and feedback concerning such learning content, class activities, and teaching strategies were kept in the teacher-researcher's field notes:

In class, when a question was posed, such as 'Who can remember what we

> have learnt from the last Chinese lesson and how to say ... in Chinese,' students acted out the interactive activity — 'Minion Says.' I noticed that most of the students raised their hands quickly to show their intention to be the 'minion' in class through speaking out the four action verbs in Chinese and working as the role of a 'Chinese teacher' in class (Field Notes, 07/03/2017).

'Minion Says' is a fun and popular activity adapted from the original form 'Simon Says,' which here was used to train the students' pronunciations and meanings concerning the Chinese vocabularies they have learnt, especially effective in practising such verbs. Furthermore, 'Minions' is the local students' preferred and familiar cartoon which they often talk about, and share with their friends and classmates in their daily school lives. Using their favourite learning activity to teach them content which interests them helps to engage the local students in Chinese lessons in all manner of behavioural, cognitive, and affective dimensions (Butler, 2011).

Another popular game was 'Charades' used in class to help them review the learned Chinese verb phrases which occurred in playing handball:

> In this interactive activity, the students have different tasks to be completed in class, such as acting out the corresponding questions, answering the given questions, recording the gaming time, holding the game cards, being the guides/ assistants outside the game, as well as being attentive to the performers and speakers in this game (Field Notes, 21/03/2017).

During the whole 'Charades' gaming process, the students need to employ clear expression and communication, as well as meaningful body language/actions. More importantly, the students need to be familiar with the pronunciations and meanings of these Chinese vocabularies. Therefore, through this group activity, both the participants and the audience were actively willing to engage in such learning content and tasks due to the activation of their visual, verbal, bodily, interpersonal, and intrapersonal intelligence modalities in class (Gardner, 1983).

As for the evaluation activity, the students' preferred drawing activity was adopted, helping them enhance their memorisation and understanding of the learned terms regarding playing handball. Such an activity requires the students to design a handball game by drawing the relevant actions, as well as using the learned Chinese words. During the whole process, it was noticed that:

> The students were really occupied when they were drawing and showed patience in practising writing the pinyin, pronunciations, and meanings of the learned Chinese words (Field Notes, 28/03/2017).

Their classroom teachers made the following comments on such learning activities:

> With the drawing, it is making sure you are allowing all different learning styles to be used in the classroom. It is a very **inclusive** way of teaching. The students prefersketching, [like] Yina, Haoxuan, and Yajing, they particularly love sketching. They really find it highly engaging (Classroom Teacher, Mr. Ke, Year 4, 28/11/2017).

Drawing and designing activities allowed all students, whether female or male, and regardless of their different learning levels and capabilities, to engage in the learning of Chinese vocabulary in class. It was notable that pupils with diverse personalities, such as the shy girls and the mischievous boys, were all active and attentive in completing such drawing and designing activities, thus mastering these Chinese expressions regarding playing handball. During this process, these students can fully exploit their talents in drawing to design a handball competition through using the learned Chinese words concerning playing handball. It is worth stating that such used Chinese linguistic terms should be written in the form of Chinese pīnyīn (拼音) beside the corresponding movements. Drawing and designing, but also practising their pronunciations through noting the words down in Chinese pīnyīn (拼音), would deepen their memorisation of the meanings. It is well-known that drawing and designing works as an effective strategy to better student engagement and learning efficacy, especially in second language learning, as it is conducive to shaping positive attitudes, improving concentration, and streamlining their learning dilemmas in a comforting and encouraging atmosphere (Rajuan & Gidoni, 2014).

Therefore, from the perspective of knowing generally how students can learn well at school, this technique makes use of their prior knowledge about such popular and familiar class activities and games, to help them review the learned Chinese vocabulary, and ensure that the students exercise their literacy skills by writing Chinese pīnyīn (拼音), all within one of their preferred instruction styles. This phenomenon is echoed by Cummins's clarification (2007) that 'the role of prior knowledge is particularly relevant to the issue of teaching for cross-linguistic transfer' (p.232), as such knowledge helps to form the students' identity and cognitive functioning' (p.232) based on the 'information or skills previously acquired in a transmission-oriented instructional sequence' (p.232). The above-mentioned instruction strategies employed in Chinese lessons do not just 'explicitly attempt to activate students' prior knowledge' (p.232) regarding these popular learning activities in the local educational milieu, but also essentially 'build relevant background knowledge as necessary' (p.232) for effecting the inclusive knowledge transfer from L1 (English) to L2 (Chinese) (Cummins, 2007).

9.1.2 Teaching Linguistic Terms Identified from Playing Ping Pong

A relevant lesson plan was designed to teach linguistic terms used in playing ping pong, which is illustrated in Table 9.2.

Table 9.2 Chinese lesson plan for teaching linguistic terms used in playing ping pong

Term 2 &Week 3 — Week 9	**Unit Title: Sports – pīngpāngqiú – 乒乓球 (ping pong)**	**Date: 09/05/2017—20/06/2017**	**Class: Year 3 & Year 4**
Expected Learning Outcomes	1. The first teaching purpose will focus on the necessary equipment used for playing ping pong. After the students get familiar with the pronunciations and meanings of such vocabulary in Chinese, authentic and interactive activities outside the classroom will be adopted to strengthen their memorisation and usage of them. 2. It is anticipated that they will then know and be familiar with how to express the scoring of ping pong in Chinese. 3. The expected learning outcomes are that the students will become familiar with the meanings and pronunciations of 'cáipàn – 裁判' (referee), 'bǐfēn – 比分' (scoring), 'xuǎnshǒu – 选手' (players) in combination with 'bǐ – 比 (:)' through the interactive process of playing 'pīngpāngqiú (乒乓球).'		

Continued

Term 2 &Week 3 — Week 9	**Unit Title: Sports – pīngpāngqiú – 乒乓球 (ping pong)**	**Date: 09/05/2017— 20/06/2017**	**Class: Year 3 & Year 4**
Lesson Outline	Class Learning Activity	Outdoor Learning Activity: The students will act as the 'tour guide' on campus to introduce the equipment used for playing 'pīngpāngqiú – 乒乓球' by using the following Chinese vocabulary:	
		Learning an Expression for Scoring, such as '1:2': In Chinese, ':' is read as 'bǐ,' we have '1 bǐ (比) 2.'	
Lesson Outline	Class Evaluation Activity	An Assessment Activity: 1. Seven students work in a group. 2. Four students act as the 'tour guide' on campus to introduce the equipment used for playing 'pīng pāng qiú – 乒乓球' by using Chinese. 3. One student acts as a 'cái pàn – 裁判' (referee) to present 'bǐfēn – 比分' (scoring) in Chinese. 4. Two students act as 'xuǎn shǒu – 选手' (players) to complete the competition under Mr. Zhao's instructions. 5. After three rounds of the competition, the 'cáipàn – 裁判' needs to present 'bǐfēn – 比分' in Chinese. *Please note that our classroom teacher, other group members, and Mr. Zhao will watch your work, and the group that performed better during the whole process of this activity will be rewarded.*	
	Teacher's Role	The teacher's role will be as an instructor and a facilitator during the process of giving a lecture and conducting the class activities separately.	

During the process of conducting such a learning activity, it was observed that:

After the pupils came to the pingpong field on the playground, they were asked to stand around the table. Then, I said, 'You are going to act as the 'tour guide'on campus to introduce the equipment used for playing pīngpāngqiú in Chinese.' Mingxu was the first pupil to raise his hand, pointing to the bats and saying 'zhè shì qiúpāi (这是球拍)' – this is the bat. Almost at the same time, Yina, a very active girl in Chinese class, raised her hand, showing her intention to be the next 'tour guide.' — The girl demonstrated her exact pronunciation for 'nà shì qiú (那是球)' — that is the ball (Field Notes, 09/05/2017).

In terms of the morpheme 'qiú – 球' (ball), by its very nature, it necessarily occurs in different kinds of ball sports. Correspondingly, they have learnt 'zú qiú – 足球' (football/soccer), 'páiqiú – 排球' (volleyball), and 'shǒuqiú – 手球' (handball), as well as the relevant actions for them, such as 'fā qiú – 发球' (serve the ball), 'pāi qiú – 拍球' (bounce the ball), 'chuán qiú – 传球' (pass the ball), 'jiē qiú – 接球' (catch the ball), 'chǎn qiú – 铲球' (tackle the ball) and 'dài qiú – 带球' (dribble the ball). Therefore, it was not difficult for them to pronounce the Chinese linguistic expressions for 'bat(s)' (qiúpāi – 球拍) and 'ball' (qiú – 球). It was apparent that this Chinese knowledge had been incorporated into their existing knowledge, allowing further fostering of meaningful learning in the Chinese class (Duff et al., 2013).

When it came to the subsequent 'campus tour guides,' their performance in figuring out the two newly-learned Chinese morphemes left a deep impression on me:

> When I asked 'Who would like to be the tour guide to introduce other equipment in Chinese?' In my eyes, it would be a little difficult for them to pronounce 'qiúwǎng – 球网' (net). However, Zixuan can pronounce it correctly, saying 'nà shì qiúwǎng – 那是球网' (that is the net). Finally, Shaoyang got the chance to introduce the 'table' for playing ping pong in Chinese. He said 'zhè shì qiútái – 这是球台' (this is the table) (Field Notes, 09/05/2017).

The classroom teacher remarked on such learning activities:

> I think that works well. Because you are aiming in phrase, and it is a good way to get a little bit of Chinese happening. So I think it is quite good to have a carrier sentence, you know, 'here is the bat,' 'here is the ball,' 'here is a table,' 'here is a player,' you know, you are just changing that word at the end. So it shows they can remember the phrase, as well as insert things they need to match to that, to a picture or something (Classroom Teacher, Ms. Shi, Year 4, 05/12/2017).

The following evidence from the teacher-researcher's field notes concerns the teaching practices regarding how to express the scoring for a ping pong game in

Chinese, such as 'bǐ (比)':

> At the beginning, Yina was chosen as the first 'cáipàn – 裁判' (referee). She can use the learned Chinese linguistic terms indicating the scoring between two 'xuǎnshǒu – 选手' (players), such as 'Mingxu got yī fēn (1分) – one point,' and Yujia got èrfēn (2 分) – two points.' After being informed that in oral Chinese 'two points' is read as 'liǎng fēn – 2分' (two points), when Mingxu got another point, she could even say 'Mingxu has got liǎng fēn – 2 分.' Following that, Yi'na continued using Chinese numbers and expressions to report the scoring by saying 'bǐfēn (比分) is liù (6) bǐ sān (3) – (6:3)' during the whole process of this activity (Field Notes, 16/05/2017).

During the process of conducting the role-play activities outside the classroom, the students remembered the knowledge learned from the previous Chinese lessons. They can build on such knowledge to help themselves be engaged in these newly-learned Chinese vocabularies quickly and correctly. During these Chinese lessons, the students showed great interest and initiative in acting as the 'tour guide' to introduce the equipment used for playing ping pong by using the learned Chinese expressions. The in-class engagement was reinforced with the help of their familiar sporting activity — playing ping pong, as well as their existing knowledge in relation to the Chinese language.

Later on, another girl was selected to be the second referee, saying that:

> 'I do not know how to express scoring in Chinese.' Instantly, Yi'na said that 'I show you how to do that.' Then, the girl — Yuting followed Yi'na's demonstration regarding the pronunciations of the frequently used Chinese numbers and the linguistic term '...bǐ(比)...' After my encouragement, she tried to present the scoring in Chinese, saying 'bǐfēn (比分) is yī (1) bǐ (比) sān (3)' (Field Notes, 16/05/2017).

The classroom teacher noticed and mentioned that:

> The students are more engaged and active, especially some students who are very shy. More importantly, two students have become experts in Chinese lessons.

They have set a good example for other students in class, helping other students engage in Chinese lessons (Classroom Teacher, Mr. Ke, Year 4, 20/06/2017).

He also added that:

I guess the big thing in particular in Chinese lessons is that they see the other kids having fun and that makes them want to engage and come down to you, doing a lot of the hands-on activities and turning learning things into games. They will be resistant and reluctant, but then when they see their friends too normally doing that, like 'Oh, little Jimmy is doing well now and I will have a go as well.' Because when they are doing it, they realise that 'Oh, I did not fail and I did not make a mistake. It is OK, I am an expert as well.' And next time, they want to do that more willingly (Classroom Teacher, Mr. Ke, Year 4, 20/06/2017).

Such students' existing knowledge retained and consolidated from the previous Chinese lessons contributes to some students becoming 'language experts' in learning Chinese. That in turn facilitates them to be willing to provide assistance to other students who have difficulty in mastering Chinese in class. As the above information illustrates, undoubtedly, the students' roles in the whole process of conducting such small group and role-play activities can be identified as 'trigger, solver, contributor, and observer' (p.41), which are similar responses to Dobao's (2016) research concerning peer interaction in small groups contributing to bettering their attainment and retention of L2 vocabulary. Even though the students tend to be 'silent observers of their peers' interaction' (Dobao, 2016, p.57) in Chinese class, their engagement and performances are outstanding based on these learning events. In particular, the opportunities for listening and speaking were increased for these 'silent learners' (Dobao, 2016, p.46) due to the mutual efforts of others in completing such team collaboration tasks in Chinese.

9.1.3 Teaching Linguistic Terms Identified from Playing Basketball

The lesson plan based on the content generated from playing basketball is presented in Table 9.3.

Table 9.3 Chinese lesson plan for teaching linguistic termsused in playing basketball

Term 3 & Week 3 — Week 8	**Unit Title: Sports – lánqiú – 篮球 (basketball)**	**Date: 15/08/2017—19/09/2017**	**Class: Year 3 & Year 5**
Expected Learning Outcomes	Initially, students are asked to search the vocabularies, including 'backboard, basketball hoop, and basketball court' by using the laptops/iPads in class in the form of working as a team. Subsequently, an assessment activity will be adopted in order to help the students review the sentence patterns 'zhè shì – 这是' (this is) and 'nà shì – 那是' (that is), as well as the Chinese vocabularies concerning the sports equipment used for playing 'lánqiú – 篮球' (basketball). In addition, to make the students familiar with the action words used in playing basketball, the TPR (Total Physical Response) teaching method will be adopted. Finally, after learning such Chinese expressions in relation to 'dǎ lánqiú – 打篮球' (play basketball) the students are expected to be able to use these Chinese vocabularies when playing basketball in school.		
Lesson Outline	Class Learning Activity Class Evaluation Activity	**Using Laptops/iPads to Search the Vocabularies regarding Sports Equipment Used for Playing Basketball:** 1. Students will be instructed to work in a team with three or four partners based on their own decisions. 2. One student will be selected as the team leader to bring the pencil case and a laptop/iPad. 3. After all the preparatory work is done, the following instructions will be given by showing one picture with the vocabularies to be searched. 4. While students are searching the vocabularies, they are encouraged to present their 'discoveries' in the form of drawing the playing materials, as well as writing down the corresponding Chinese pīnyīn (拼音) on A3 paper. An Assessment Activity: 1. Five students work in a group. 2. Four students act as the 'tour guide' to introduce the equipment used for playing lánqiú – 篮球 by using Chinese sentences like 这是 (This is)/那是 (That is)... 3. One student acts as the 'cáipàn – 裁判' (referee) to give instructions in Chinese such as: ...qǐng – 请 (please)... 4. The other four students act out these actions in order to finish a mini-basketball game.	

Continued

Term 3 & Week 3 — Week 8	Unit Title: Sports – lánqiú – 篮球 (basketball)	Date: 15/08/2017—19/09/2017	Class: Year 3 & Year 5
Teacher's Role		The teacher's role will be as an instructor and a facilitator during the process of giving a lecture and conducting the class activities separately.	

Initially, the students' in-class engagement and performance through using laptops/iPads to search the vocabularies in relation to the sports equipment used for playing basketball were reflected in the teacher-researcher's field notes, as shown below:

> In just a minute, Pengfei's team raised their hands and informed me that they had found out 'backboard' was pronounced as 'bèibǎn.' I responded to him that 'bǎn is correct, so please search [for] it again.' After a second, he showed me again with 'lánbǎn.' This time I said that 'It is completely right' and I gave his team a 'jiāyóu (加油)' sticker as a reward for their good efforts, encouraging them to continue working hard (Field Notes, 15/08/2017).

According to one of the classroom teachers:

> They love technology, anything that you give them, a laptop, once again they'll love it. Technology is good because everyone is really engaged in that (Classroom Teacher, Ms. Li, Year 5, 19/09/2017).

It is worth mentioning that Pengfei is a really naughty student at school. However, his engagement and behaviour in these Chinese lessons were entirely beyond the teacher-researcher's expectations. Pengfei's team was The first group to complete this learning task and under his leadership.

There was also an extremely shy girl — Yajing in my Chinese class. She never raised her hand to answer any questions, but she always listened to the lectures carefully in class and was always willing to participate in the activities needed to work as a team, including drawing, designing, writing, paper folding, and cutting activities conducted in Chinese lessons. When being asked to pronounce one of the Chinese vocabularies that she had searched with other team members, the following happened:

> She shook her head slightly, indicating her refusal to do that. So I asked Manni in her team to speak them out in Chinese. She was active in presenting their search results in front of the class. As for the last word — 'lánqiú (篮球)' – basketball, I mentioned 'Please say it in Chinese together.' I noticed that Yajing opened her mouth and said that word in Chinese with other partners in her team together. At the same time, their team not only showed fabulous writing and skillful speaking of these illustrated vocabularies, but also demonstrated their vivid drawing for these corresponding searched Chinese words (Field Notes, 15/08/2017).

During this entire exercise, it was noted that most of the students were trying their best to pronounce these searched Chinese vocabularies by using the pronunciation function in Google Translation, rather than just asking the teacher how to pronounce them or telling the teacher that they cannot do that before presenting their search results. Their classroom teachers provided the following views regarding such teaching strategy:

> Using the technology to incorporate into the Chinese lessons gives them a little independence. And I think every kid no matter who they are, will get a lot of information from them, they are already engaged in. In these activities ahead, I think it is good to incorporate these laptops and the internet so they can learn more (Classroom Teacher, Ms. Mu, Year 5, 21/11/2017).
>
> I think they really like that. Using technology is very important. And it also increases students' engagement. So they are very interested in what they are doing, especially when they are using an iPad. It allows them to find out what they would like to know about, which is really good (Classroom Teacher, Ms. Shen, Year 3, 07/12/2017).

As the above evidence demonstrates, the local school students have a strong capability in using advanced technology to develop their independent learning in various subjects. This local public school also provides easy access for the students to use iPads, laptops, and computers, which is aimed at cultivating their learning interests and abilities so that they can undertake future study on their own. The local students at this school are fond of and skillful in utilising such advanced technology to assist them in learning languages, science, history, geography, art, and mathematics, so it is no surprise that they employ this kind of learning in Chinese class. Letting the students themselves shoulder more responsibilities, or 'be the leaders,' in the fields which they are experts, or with which they are most familiar, can activate and mobilise their powerful knowledge shaped from real-life practices.

Here, that means making use of their powerful knowledge of using such digital learning devices as the funds of knowledge for bettering their learning of Chinese (Roth & Erstad, 2013; Schuck, Kearney & Burden, 2017). This phenomenon echoes the belief that the utilisation of advanced technology for students' foreign language learning can alter the process of their knowledge gaining, due in part to the repeated retrieval of online vocabulary dictionaries on their own, thus impacting their engagement and information retention in terms of greater self-fulfillment and independence (Golonka, Bowles, Frank, Richardson & Freynik, 2014).

Meanwhile, strengthening opportunities to have them work in the form of a team can lessen their sense of lacking security or belonging, and alleviate their shyness to a certain extent. That is to say, allocating different roles for each team member in a group helps them to form a sense of ownership during the process of Chinese language learning. The students in this study certainly exploited their powerful knowledge in using advanced technology, as well as their prior knowledge in drawing and designing, to support and cooperate with each other in a team, which made them more engaged with the learning content.

Subsequently, the total physical response (TPR) teaching method was adopted to help the students learn the action verbs which frequently occurred in playing basketball through giving them instructions in Chinese, such as 'Please chuán qiú – (传球), jiē qiú – (接球), yùn qiú – (运球) and tóulán – (投篮).' After one round, the students were instructed to sit in a circle on the floor in class and one student was selected to give instructions in Chinese standing in the middle of them. When they gradually got familiar with this activity and could give instructions in Chinese fluently on their own, it was apparent that:

> They can use the language, such as 'Please chuán qiú (传球) to ... ' making

up a complete sentence by their own thinking, not just a verb phrase. When it came to the action 'shoot' (tóulán – 投篮), some students, such as Pengfei, Shaoyang and Mingxu acted as the basketball hoop (lánkuāng – 篮筐) for the 'players' to shoot by crossing their two arms to form a hoop (Field Notes, 05/09/2017).

Their classroom teacher explained:

> I think that they really enjoyed their hands-on activities when you got actual, physical, like the cards they can hold and say the words on the cards, throwing the ball around (Classroom Teacher, Ms. Li, Year 5, 19/09/2017).

By its very nature of being an action term, total physical response (TPR) allowed the students to perform and practise such verbs as occurred in playing basketball through their body language. A case in point was that the local students demonstrated their exact understanding of 'tóulán – 投篮' (shoot) by acting as the 'basketball hoop' (lánkuāng – 篮筐) for the 'players' to shoot. Also, the process of performing such hands-on activity among the students helped to mobilise their existing sports-related Chinese expressions learned and sustained from the previous Chinese lessons.

In terms of the assessment activity for the topic concerning playing basketball, students were required to act as the 'tour guide' to introduce the sports equipment used for playing basketball in Chinese with the two basic learned Chinese sentence patterns, namely 'zhè shì – 这是' (this is) and 'nà shì – 那是' (that is). After that, they were asked to apply the four basic action verbs which occurred in playing basketball into a real situation — performing a mini-basketball game. Meanwhile, the vocabulary 'cáipàn – 裁判' (referee) was again introduced into this assessment activity. One student played the role of a 'cáipàn – 裁判,' giving different instructions in Chinese. The other students in the same team needed to act out the corresponding actions. In class, it was observed that:

> Without using flashcards to remind them of the vocabularies for sports equipment, including 'lánbǎn (篮板), lánkuāng (篮筐), lánqiú chǎng (篮球场) and lánqiú (篮球),' a few students, such as Mingxu, Wenjie, Junwei, Xinyi, Yi'na,

and Ya'nan can remember and pronounce such vocabularies in Chinese very well. Now and then, they also gave some hints to their team members on how to say them in Chinese in a whisper (Field Notes, 19/09/2017).

Under the guidance from 'cáipàn – 裁判' and assistance from team members, this assessment activity was conducted smoothly and completed successfully, achieving the anticipated learning outcomes to a certain extent. Subsequently, one of their classroom teachers gave the following remarks on such a teaching strategy:

> The outdoor activity, is a fantastic way of learning in any subject. And it is worth absolutely using that in Chinese as well. And the children enjoy that activity. They enjoy the basketball activity. They use that in the playground when they are playing there. You know, they would use the vocabulary as well. So it is really good. Taking children outside, they generally are more engaged, they are excited about the learning, and they enjoy that more (Classroom Teacher, Ms. Shěn, Year 3, 07/12/2017).

Students commented on such a hands-on activity:

> Yujia: I think it is very cool, because we actually go outside, and like [to] see the things on the basketball court that we would more say in English. Now we can say them in two languages to show the class how we can say the main two languages. Ruxue: I think it is very fun to play basketball in Chinese words because it is a wholly new thing for people who do not know Chinese (Focus Group A, Year 3, 07/12/2017).

The expected learning outcomes of this assessment activity were for the students to use the above-mentioned two Chinese sentences to practise the pronunciations of the vocabularies in relation to the basketball sports equipment in a real situation, viewing the concrete objects. Carrying out such a miniature basketball match in Chinese class is also beneficial in getting students familiar with the pronunciations and meanings of the four verb phrases which frequently occur in playing basketball through acting out corresponding movements. In this regard, to develop pupils' vocabulary learning proficiency in EFL, it is suggested that the role-play activity, as a technique, should be included in any English course construction (Alabsi, 2016). Successfully transferring such a strategy into Chinese language classrooms, by its essential nature, demonstrates its effectiveness and achievement in teaching the local school students such Chinese expressions in relation to playing basketball, which helps to create joyful learning experiences and outstanding learning outcomes in such an authentic learning environment.

Based on the information from the teacher-researcher's daily field notes, as well as the feedback from students and their classroom teachers, it is clear that the above-mentioned learning activities, such as 'Minion Says,' 'Charades,' 'Drawing & Designing,' 'Using Advanced Technology,' as well as 'Outdoor Interactive & Role-Play Activities' are well-known and favoured among the local students for mastering different subjects at school. As the four-character Chinese metaphor 'xǐwénlèjiàn – 喜闻乐见' suggests, these local students are very engaged in the Chinese teaching content through participating in such school-based learning activities, which they are extremely familiar with and fond of. Undertaking such students''xǐwénlèjiàn – 喜闻乐见' activities can be another essential route for the Chinese teacher-researcher to gain awareness regarding how to organise and enrich their learning of Chinese in the local educational milieu.

9.2 Lǎnglǎngshàngkǒu – 朗朗上口[1] melody

The relevant lesson plan with regard to how to teach the expression 'Happy birthday to you' in Chinese, is displayed in Table 9.4.

1 The original source of the Chinese version: 老舍《诗与快板 》:"散文就不受这么多的限制，虽然散文也讲究声调铿锵，能朗朗上口。" Originally, it refers to a genre with certain rhythms, such as verse or poetry, which is easy to read aloud and remember the content.

Table 9.4 Lesson plan for teaching 'Happy birthday to you' in Chinese

Term 3 & Week 4 — Week 8	**Unit Title: Singing – zhùnǐ shēngrì kuàilè – 祝你生日快乐(Happy birthday to you)**		**Date: 29/08/2017—19/09/2017**	**Class: Year 3, Year 4 & Year 5**
Expected Learning Outcomes	Initially, the students are expected to be able to sing 'Happy birthday to you' in Chinese while a song video with the Chinese lyrics is being played in class. Following that, they are expected to be able to sing 'Happy birthday to you' in Chinese while the corresponding melody of the birthday song is being played in class. Gradually, students are able to say the Chinese expression 'zhù nǐ shēngrì kuàilè -祝你生日快乐,' which they can use for the purpose of giving good wishes during their classmates', teachers', friends' and parents' birthdays.			
Lesson Outline	Class Learning Activity & Class Evaluation Activity	Firstly, the song video with Chinese lyrics is going to be repeatedly played at the very beginning of each Chinese lesson in order to get them familiar with the Chinese pronunciation and meaning of 'zhùnǐ shēngrì kuàilè – 祝你生日快乐.' Subsequently, they will be instructed in learning the content concerning how to express 'Happy birthday to you' in the Chinese way. Progressively, after they have become familiar with the pronunciation and meaning of 'zhùnǐ shēngrì kuàilè – 祝你生日快乐,' the corresponding melody of that birthday song will be repeatedly played at the very beginning of each Chinese lesson to help them practice singing and saying 'Happy birthday to you' in Chinese.		
Teacher's Role	The teacher's role will be as an instructor and a facilitator during the process of giving a lecture and conducting the class activities separately.			

During this activity, it was observed that:

At the very beginning of the Chinese lesson, the students were informed that they would listen to a Chinese birthday song with both the Chinese lyrics and the English meanings. During the process of listening, I found that some students tended to sing this Chinese birthday song with that video in their low voices. After the Chinese birthday song had been repeated twice in the video, I passed the microphone to Tianlei and then to Haoxuan. They can sing it well in Chinese (Field Notes, 29/08/2017).

An impressive moment happened in one of these classes:

> As normal, when I entered the classroom, I asked 'Is there anyone's birthday today?' All the students in class responded to me loudly with 'Today is Jingqi's birthday.' At that time, I just was ready to lead them to review how to say 'Happy birthday' in Chinese and sing that song again. Afterwards, I said 'Now please let us say 'shēngrì kuàilè' to Jingqi together.' Then, I encouraged them to sing that birthday song to her together in Chinese while such melody was being played. Meanwhile, Jingqi was invited to the front, singing with us. To my delight, they really sang it well in Chinese and can still remember the meaning of 'shēngrì kuàilè.' I cannot forget the warm and enjoyable scene in which they sang the song 'Happy Birthday to You' in Chinese (Field Notes, 12/09/2017).

Another unforgettable situation occurred in Chinese class at the end of this term, a performance by the ten boys:

> In this lesson, I also led them to review the Chinese birthday song together. The ten boys put their arms on each other's shoulders and waved their bodies while they were singing the song in Chinese. It was really a warm learning environment in class by using such a catchy and well-known song in their daily life (Field Notes, 19/09/2017).

A bond with reciprocal support between the learners of the Chinese language and the Chinese teacher-researcher had been created in class. That was a learning environment imbued with warmth, joy, and especially with a sense of self-security which can be easily constructed among these students. As for the significance of using songs for language acquisition, it has been stressed by Candlin (1992) that 'songs have a place in the classroom for helping create that friendly and co-operative atmosphere so important for language learning' (p.ix). Namely, this rapport and the harmonious class atmosphere were helpful for the local students in promoting their chances of using 'zhùnǐ shēngrì kuàilè – 祝你生日快乐' (Happy birthday to you) during the school celebratory practice. After class, their classroom teachers made such comments on using the well-known birthday melody to engage them in the learning of a Chinese birthday expression, as follows:

> It is really a fun and stress-free way. It does not reflect your answers, because

they have already sung 'Happy Birthday.' Harmoniously, the shy ones (especially some girls), when they saw the loud group of boys being silly doing it, they started joining them as well. So it takes the pressure away from them, and it encourages them to engage with the students as well, very participative. They have learnt the song in a sort of singing lesson – it is the Chinese language lesson with the tune they have known (Classroom Teacher, Mr. Ke, Year 4, 28/11/2017).

The 'Happy Birthday' is quite handy because we do sing 'Happy Birthday' in class. And it is a kind of a song everyone knows. So it is nice to know it in another language. Because using the same melody...because it is the same melody, it helps them to connect and engage. Because they know, [like] 'Oh, I know the song, I know that tune, I know the melody.' So they are more interested in learning it, they know it in English. So to them, it is really close for them to know in Chinese. 'So when mum has a birthday I can sing "Happy Birthday" in Chinese.' It gives them something to connect to Chinese, too. And the tune would often help them remember the lyrics (Classroom Teacher, Ms. Shi, Year 4, 05/12/2017).

The students really enjoyed learning Chinese in this way:

(Haoxuan) Because they really, really, know the song fully. So overall, I think it is a good strategy. (Ya'nan) I like the birthday song because the song it is good. It is really catchy (Focus Group C, Year 5, 21/11/2017).

As the above evidence shows, the local school students already have a strong knowledge basis for singing the song titled 'Happy Birthday to You' in English due to their daily frequent exposures to that song's lyrics and tune. That is to say, knowing this world-renowned birthday song's melody is another embodiment of the local students' prior knowledge that has been picked up and retained from their daily birthday celebratory happenings. Particularly, such an example of prior knowledge can be considered as one of their funds of knowledge that has been shaped for a long period and derived from the birthday celebration practice. The students' prior knowledge concerning the catchy birthday melody also suits the birthday song with Chinese lyrics. Namely, the Chinese version of that popular birthday song shares the same tune with the English one, which is also memorable.

Accordingly, as the four-character Chinese metaphor 'lǎnglǎngshàngkǒu' (朗朗上口) indicates, the Chinese birthday song, with its attractive cadence, is also easy for the local school students to sing aloud, and it is easy to remember the content based on the exploitation of their prior knowledge in relation to the appealing melody. Clearly, during the process of learning how to sing and say 'Happy birthday to you' in Chinese, a novel classroom routine has been established in Chinese class. Explicitly, the singing of the song entitled 'zhùnǐ shēngrì kuàilè – 祝你生日快乐' at the very beginning of each Chinese lesson. Such a classroom routine was established voluntarily, and performed habitually by the students in class, although this had not been planned by the Chinese teacher-researcher. Furthermore, the local school students' prior knowledge of this catchy melody was not restricted by their gender, as both genders of students had already developed such knowledge of that song. Correspondingly, their built-up knowledge and reinforced confidence in having been familiar with such a popular tune not only contributed to enhancing both female and male students' mutual engagement in Chinese class, but also constructed a warm space for their learning of Chinese in school.

Therefore, employing the strategy of the 'lǎnglǎngshàngkǒu' (朗朗上口) melody enriches the opportunities for the local students to use 'zhùnǐ shēngrì kuàilè' (祝你生日快乐) in their daily lives. By doing so, they can strongly manifest their translanguaging capability between English and Chinese. Such ability is reinforced particularly when their prior knowledge of singing the English birthday song has been activated and transferred for learning the new Chinese expression — 'zhùnǐ shēngrì kuàilè' (祝你生日快乐). As their emergent bilinguals become validated and consolidated, the students would unsurprisingly transform their identity in order to engage and maintain such newly-learned knowledge in their habituated circumstance (Creese & Blackledge, 2010; Lave & Wenger, 1991). In addition, the friendship among the students is strengthened, helping build a supportive Chinese learning environment in school due partly to their joint involvement in Chinese class. However, it should be mentioned that given the gender influence behind affection for particular music styles, it is important to perhaps re-orientate the content and employ genres of music which both genders enjoy or the more familiar songs everyone enjoys, such as 'Happy Birthday to You.'

9.3 Rónghuìguàntōng – 融会贯通[1]

The following lesson plan (Table 9.5) concentrates on the teaching content in relation to making mathematical calculations in Chinese, followed by the collected information from the teacher-researcher's daily teaching practices.

Table 9.5 Lesson plan for teaching mathematical calculations in Chinese

Term 4 & Week 2 —Week 6	**Unit Title: Calculating – jìsuàn – 计算 (calculation)**		**Date: 17/10/2017—17/11/2017**	**Class: Year 3, Year 4 & Year 5**
Expected Learning Outcomes	1. Make the students familiar with the pronunciations and meanings of the five basic calculation symbols in Chinese through using the learned Chinese numbers to complete basic and simple mathematical calculations. 2. Adopting a game entitled 'Magic Time' to help the students get more familiar with the pronunciations and meanings of the five basic calculation symbols in Chinese. 3. After a period of learning, they are expected to be able to do calculations in Chinese skillfully outside Chinese class or school, in daily life, or maybe later in China.			
Lesson Outline	Learning Activityvs Evaluation Activity	Make a Guess for the Chosen Calculation Symbol(s): Use the dice, as well as the flashcards with numbers and calculation symbols. Throw one dice to get one number. Throw another dice to get another number. After that, the corresponding calculation symbols, including 'jiā (加), jiǎn (减), chéng (乘), chú (除), and děngyú (等于)' will be chosen to complete a mathematical calculation, while using the number flashcards to indicate the final result. Please remember that the numbers you got and the calculation symbols you chose are required to be said in Chinese.		

1 The original source of the Chinese version:《朱子全书·学三 》:"举一而三反，闻一而知十，乃学者用功之深，穷理之熟，然后能融会贯通，以至于此。" In the Chinese sense: 融会：融合领会；贯通：贯穿前后。把各方面的知识和道理融化汇合，得到全面透彻的理解。In English, it refers to achieving the mastery of new knowledge through combining it with the existing knowledge comprehensively.

Continued

<table>
<tr><th>Term 4 & Week 2 —Week 6</th><th>Unit Title: Calculating – jìsuàn – 计算 (calculation)</th><th>Date: 17/10/2017— 17/11/2017</th><th>Class: Year 3, Year 4 & Year 5</th></tr>
<tr><td>Lesson Outline</td><td>Learning Activity vs Evaluation Activity</td><td colspan="2">Magic Time:
A piece of cloth will be used to cover all the five flashcards with calculation symbols. Meanwhile, the flashcards with numbers will be put into a big bag. You need to close your eyes while these preparation tasks are being done.
Afterwards, one corresponding flashcard will be taken away.
Next, you can open your eyes and one of you will be selected to guess which is on the missing flashcard.
Subsequently, please use the symbol that has been taken away to complete a mathematical calculation.
Please remember that you are required to use Chinese to do all the above-mentioned tasks.</td></tr>
<tr><td colspan="2">Teacher's Role</td><td colspan="2">The teacher's role will be as an instructor and a facilitator during the process of giving a lecture and conducting the class activities separately.</td></tr>
</table>

Before conducting the first learning activity, the students were instructed to sit in a circle on the floor. Two different dices, as well as the flashcards with calculation symbols of corresponding pronunciations, were prepared. Firstly, a demonstration from the Chinese teacher was presented to the students to make them aware of the rules of this activity. Afterwards, the students were advised to work as a team to complete the corresponding task. In terms of their involvement, it was found that:

> One group of students got two '6' after throwing two dices separately. Then, they preferred to choose 'jiā (加)' as the symbol for such calculation. However, they raised their hands, suggesting not knowing how to express numbers beyond '10' in Chinese (Field Notes, 17/10/2017).

That provided me with a good opportunity for developing their numeracy abilities to say more numbers in Chinese. Subsequently, I added:

> Now, please follow Mr. Zhao to count numbers starting from 11 (shíyī) in Chinese. We counted from 11 (shíyī) to 19 (shíjiǔ), showing them how to combine the learned Chinese numbers into the newly-learned ones, such as '10 (shí) along with 1 (yī), we got 11 (shíyī).' When it comes to '20 (èrshí),' I said

that 'we are going to learn it in the following Chinese lessons.' Immediately, Haoxuan, a boy said 'èrshí.' I continued asking him 'How do you know that?' Then, he responded that 'You have taught us how to say the numbers from 0 to 10 in Chinese, such as '2' is pronounced as 'èr,' '10' is pronounced as 'shí,' so I think that it is pronounced as 'èrshí' (Field Notes, 17/10/2017).

Subsequently, in order to get students more familiar with the learned five basic calculation symbols together with the learned numbers in Chinese the learning activity entitled 'Magic Time' was adopted. As for the first round, the flashcards with five calculation symbols were distributed randomly on the floor in the middle of the classroom, covering them with a cloth. Meanwhile, students could not open their eyes until one of the flashcards had been taken away.

They raised their hands so quickly, indicating to answer this question actively and confidently. Pengfei got the first opportunity to find out the missing calculation symbol, and told us it in Chinese. He said that quickly and exactly 'It is chú (除) that has been taken away' (Field Notes, 31/10/2017).

Afterwards, all the numbers from 0 to 10 were put into a big bag. One of the students was invited to pick up one number randomly from the big bag, speaking it out in Chinese:

The first number Jingqi got was 'shí (10).' The second number was 'jiǔ (9),' which was obtained from Haoxuan's random selection. They can pronounce the two numbers in Chinese very well (Field Notes, 31/10/2017).

When it came to the final result, the students encountered a situation: Was that 'shí (10) chú (除) jiǔ (9) děngyú (等于) …?'

They said to themselves in whispers 'shí chú jiǔ děngyú…?' or 'jiǔ chú shí děngyú…?' After thinking for a while, Pengfei told me 'jiǔ chú shí děngyú 0.9.' Very quickly, he picked up '0 and 9' from these numbers on the floor (Field Notes, 31/10/2017).

In terms of the second round, the students were informed that this 'Magic

Game' would be played in another way. At the very beginning of the second round, one of the students was selected to give instructions for this game in the middle of the classroom:

> This time, the first selected student was Tianmei, and it was suggested she put the five flashcards with calculation symbols into that big bag. Then, she asked one of her classmates to randomly take one out of the bag, which was 'jiā.' The two Chinese numbers were also got in the same way. Subsequently, such mathematical calculation was completed 'shí (10) jiā (加) liù (6) děngyú (等于) shíliù (16)' (Field Notes, 31/10/2017).

After the numbers, such as 11, 12, 13, 14, 15, and 16 repeatedly occurred in the final calculation result, it was found that:

> The students tended to be more familiar with these numbers' Chinese pronunciations. At first, they just pronounced them as 'yī yī,' 'yī èr.' ... Based on several practices of such numbers that occurred in the calculation results, most of them can pronounce them as 'shíyī (11), shíèr (12), ... shíliù (16)' through using the learned Chinese numbers and calculation symbols to make some mathematical calculations during Chinese lessons (Field Notes, 31/10/2017).

As for the last round, in order to make more students engaged in the learning activity, the five flashcards with calculation symbols were secretly put in front of five students while they were closing their eyes. Before that, the five numbers, including 10 (shí), 2 (èr), 3 (sān), 8 (bā), 5 (wǔ) had been written down on a whiteboard, to be used for making a little complicated mathematical calculation. After the five students got the corresponding calculation symbols, they were invited to the front, mutually negotiating and thinking together to figure out a final result. During the whole process, they were advised to use the learnt Chinese knowledge as much as possible. It was noticeable that in such a process the five students were able to use the learned Chinese linguistic terms as much as they could remember to discuss them, arranging the different calculation symbols into their proper positions. The students said:

> 'děngyú(等于) should come to the position in front of the final result,'

'jiā (加) should be put to the position before the number 'bā (8),' 'it is better to put "jiǎn(减)" into the second position for calculation symbol,' 'chú(除) must be put to the position before the number wǔ (5),' and then 'chéng(乘) comes to the first position for the calculation symbol — between shí (10) and èr (2).' They discussed again and again how to complete such a little complicated mathematical calculation in Chinese. Finally, the calculating process and the final result were presented on the whiteboard (Field Notes, 31/10/2017).

The whole process of making such calculations was being conducted and finally completed through their mutual efforts in a team, which not only helped the students advance their individual engagement in practising the pronunciations of the newly-learned Chinese vocabularies, but also turned out to be effective in mobilising their multi-intelligences, including doing, speaking, as well as thinking, especially when learning Chinese in such a monolingual (English-speaking) space.

Following the students' in-class engagement and performance regarding learning the five basic calculation symbols, and building on the learned Chinese numbers from 0 to 10, their classroom teachers similarly indicated that:

It is a very effective strategy. Because it allows students to revise things they already know, so it is extra practise. And also it gives them confidence in learning new things, because they are using vocabulary, words, or knowledge they already have to engage with something new which will be challenging for them. It makes that link for them, and gives them a connection to what they already know (Classroom Teacher, Mr. Ke, Year 4, 28/11/2017).

Oh, you need to do that, you need to be springboarding from what they know to learn more. So you should be doing that, building on each thing. So you start by learning, you know the numbers, and once we know those numbers, we can count one to ten, then we can add the math symbols, and then we can make little number sentences. So you do need to be using those building steps (Classroom Teacher, Ms. Shi, Year 4, 05/12/2017).

They learn very well when you build on what they already know. That is very helpful. And with the numbers as well, they were able to because they learned the numbers, they learnt the equation so they were able to pick up them [these activities] very well. One thing must be built on...ah, so they can continue getting better and better. So that is really good. They found it easier as well. That is to say, they are more engaged. It is not too hard for them where ... If we just started, just try to teach them sentences straight away, it would be too much. They would not understand it. Because they already knew the numbers, we were able to teach them sentences more effectively (Classroom Teacher, Ms. Shen, Year 3, 07/12/2017).

The teacher-researcher's practices of teaching mathematical calculation symbols combined with the learned Chinese numbers, as well as the feedback from the classroom teachers, revealed that focusing on the concept of 'rónghuìèguàntōng' (融会贯通) can enable the local students to activate their existing knowledge that had been retained from the previous Chinese lessons, thus making it part of their funds of knowledge formed in the school-based community. Here, it is emphasised that the existing knowledge of the local students is specified as their learned knowledge of Chinese numbers from 0 to 10. Additionally, the local students' knowledge in relation to doing mathematical calculations with the basic symbols is another embodiment of their prior knowledge that supports them to be engaged in the learning of Chinese calculation symbols and more Chinese numbers (from 11 to 20) in class. Also, to make a balanced link between students' prior and existing knowledge to the mastery of new information, it is argued that teachers not only should offer effective instruction strategies to complete such forward knowledge transfer, for instance, utilising their prior and existing knowledge to obtain the new knowledge, but should also recognise the potential impacts of backward information transfer, namely employing newly-learned knowledge to enhance their memorisation of the previously-learned information (Hohensee, 2016).

As the nature of 'rónghuìguàntōng' (融会贯通) suggests, the local students' existing knowledge about the learned Chinese numbers, as well as their prior knowledge on the general calculation rules, collectively prepare them to achieve new and challenging language knowledge, namely the five calculation symbols in Chinese and the Chinese numbers beyond 10. The extent of such student knowledge is not determined by gender. That is to say, both boys and girls have already mastered the basic rules of making mathematical calculations in English, attributable to their daily access to learning activities for cultivating their numeracy expertise in school. At the same time, these groups of students have been exposed to the learning of Chinese for a period of time in school, especially the Chinese numbers. That means not only did these students already know how to make mathematical calculations, but they were also already familiar with these Chinese numbers (from 0 to 10). Consequently, combining the five newly-learned mathematical calculation symbols with the formerly-learned Chinese numbers and mathematical equations advances these students' capabilities to attain such new Chinese linguistic terms on calculations and more Chinese numbers, in a way which minimises pressure.

On the other hand, 'rónghuìguàntōng' (融会贯通) becomes a tool for identifying and utilising other forms of the local students' funds of knowledge in school, such as their prior knowledge of the basic calculation principles, and existing knowledge of the learned Chinese numbers, that would help to consolidate their learning of the novel Chinese language knowledge relevant to the mathematical calculation symbols. In this way, the students in the class are actively absorbed in these learning activities, not being 'ignorant and passive puppets.' Naturally, such knowledge is essentially in the course of getting the local students to initiate their learning of the new and thought-provoking Chinese knowledge, for instance, the Chinese expressions of the basic calculation symbols. Through employing the local students' funds of knowledge shaped in the school-based community, the teacher-researcher complies with the notion of 'rónghuìguàntōng' (融会贯通) that deepens the understanding of the local students' intellectual repertoires, which can contribute to their further learning achievements in Chinese language.

Therefore, based on the concept of 'rónghuìèguàntōng' (融会贯通), it is clear that the local school students are capable of pronouncing and making sensing of the five newly-learned Chinese calculation symbols, together with the learned Chinese numbers, through making mathematical calculations by themselves in Chinese. It has also been proved that as the students get more familiar with such knowledge, they gradually develop their translanguaging capabilities in mastering more new Chinese knowledge by their own, through effecting the benefits brought by 'rónghuìguàntōng' (融会贯通).

9.4 Huìshēnghuìsè – 绘声绘色[1]

This subsection presents a lesson plan (Table 9.6) in relation to teaching the corresponding Chinese linguistic expressions for the English words which students frequently use for their daily shopping at the school canteen.

Table 9.6 Lesson plan for teaching shopping in Chinese

Term 4 & Week 4 — Week 9	**Unit Title: School Canteen Shopping – gòuwù – 购物 (shopping)**	**Date: 31/10/2017—05/12/2017**	**Class: Year 3, Year 4 & Year 5**
Expected Learning Outcomes (Listening & Speaking)	Initially, a 'drama performing' activity is designed and employed to help the students develop their initial cognition towards the pronunciations and meanings of the Chinese linguistic expressions which correspond to the English they employ while shopping at the school canteen. Subsequently, a matching activity is adopted to judge their understanding concerning the pronunciations and meanings of such Chinese sentences used for their daily shopping activity. Afterwards, the following learning activities, namely 'You Draw, I Guess' and 'Picking Mushrooms' (cǎi mógu – 采蘑菇) will be carried out to help them get more familiar with the pronunciations and meanings of vocabularies concerning the top three most popular foods at the school canteen, including 'ròubǐng (肉饼) – meat pie,' 'shòusī (寿司) – sushi roll(s),' 'chǎo fàn (炒饭) – Chinese fried rice,' as well as the frequently used Chinese sentence patterns for shopping as the above shown. After a period of learning, students are expected to be able to perform shopping in Chinese class, or in their daily lives outside Chinese class, or maybe later shopping in China.		

1 The original source of the Chinese version: 清·朱庭珍《筱园诗话 》卷一："必使山情水性，因绘声绘色而曲得其真；务期天巧地灵，借人工人第而华传其妙。" 本义是把人物的声音、神色都描绘出来。形容叙述、描写生动逼真。绘：描绘，描摹。 It originally means that something is described in a very vivid way and lifelike style through presenting its sound and appearance.

Continued

Term 4 & Week 4 — Week 9	**Unit Title: School Canteen Shopping – gòuwù – 购物 (shopping)**	**Date: 31/10/2017—05/12/2017**	**Class: Year 3, Year 4 & Year 5**
Lesson Outline	Learning Activity vs. Evaluation Activity	Drama Performing — Shopping in Chinese: Two students work in pairs. One student acts as the buyer. The other student acts as the sales person. Acting out this real shopping situation in Chinese by using the provided menu.	
		You Draw, I Guess: Two students work in pairs. One student needs a draw a picture based on the given instructions/clues from Mr. Zhao. The other student will make a guess about the drawn picture, namely tell us what it is in Chinese. The two students who use the least time to answer it correctly will be the winning group.	
		Picking Mushrooms (cǎi mógu – 采蘑菇): According to the instructions that you heard from Mr. Zhao or your classmates, please pick the correct mushroom. A demonstration will be given to you: Please pick a 'hóngsè' (红色) mushroom for 'nǐ hǎo, wǒ yào yī gè shòusī' (你好，我要一个寿司), then please quickly put a hóngsè (红色) mushroom beside that sentence. After finishing picking all the different coloured mushrooms, the students need to put the flashcard with the corresponding English meaning of each Chinese sentence beside each mushroom.	
Teacher's Role		The teacher's role will be as an instructor and a facilitator during the process of giving a lecture and conducting the class activities separately.	

In order to get the students familiar with the pronunciations and meanings of the Chinese linguistic expressions which correspond to the English they use in their daily shopping practice at the school canteen, the following learning and teaching strategy was adopted to construct a real shopping situation in class:

One student acted as the sales person, and another student was invited to be the buyer. Meanwhile, the apron, the Chinese menu, the Chinese currency, and the food flashcards were well-prepared. Subsequently, the shopping dialogue began with a sentence, such as 'Hello, Can I have a Sushi Roll?' followed by 'Sure, that would be three dollars.' That continued with 'Here you are,' 'Here is your Sushi Roll,' and ended with 'Thanks, as well as Bye-bye.' It was noticed that when being asked to perform this shopping situation in English, almost all the students were active to raise their hands, showing me their preference and willingness to participate in this activity (Field Notes, 07/11/2017).

Such drama performances in English were conducted among the three groups. It was then time to transfer their attention to the Chinese sentence patterns while they were concentrating on this activity. After that, they were instructed and encouraged to act it out in Chinese by using the sentences shown to them. The first demonstration was performed by the Chinese teacher-researcher in cooperation with one of the students. On the one hand, this was intended to give students a better understanding of this learning task. On the other hand, it helped them regarding their cognition towards the pronunciations and meanings of the corresponding Chinese sentences used for this shopping practice. During their performances, it was noticed that:

> The students were really skilful in pronouncing such Chinese linguistic expressions as 'nǐhǎo (你好), xièxie (谢谢), and zàijiàn (再见).' They can even say them in Chinese naturally. After two rounds, I said 'Now, two students will be invited to the front to act it out in Chinese, the team that performs well will get the stickers as the awards from me.' Just at that point, both boys and girls were really active and joyful to be involved in this learning activity. They were not scared of using the Chinese language to perform this real shopping situation in class. Even though Péng Fēi initially inquired that 'Can I use English to act it out?' he then asked 'Can we do it in Chinese outside class?' (Field Notes, 07/11/2017).

Such questions informed the Chinese teacher-researcher that this kind of learning style can really help the students more readily to use the Chinese language for shopping activities inside school and outside school. Subsequently, the students were selected to work in pairs to act out the real shopping situation in Chinese with the help of the Chinese money, the Chinese menu, the food flashcards, as well as the apron, recorded as follows:

> They tended to use 'shòusī (寿司)' as the food they would like to buy. After two rounds, I announced that 'shòusī (寿司) has been sold out, please choose the other food to buy' (Field Notes, 07/11/2017).
>
> Later, Yujia from the third group, said **'nǐhǎo (你好), wǒ yào yī gè ròubǐng (我要一个肉饼)?'** (Hello, Can I have a meat pie?). And then, the boy — Mingxu in the final group said that **'nǐhǎo (你好), wǒ yào yī gè chǎofàn** (我要一个炒饭)?' (Hello, Can I have the fried rice?), adding 'I like eating chǎofàn' (Field Notes, 07/11/2017).

As for the sentence pattern 'zhè shì (这是) – here is/this is' which occurred in the shopping language, it was observed and worth mentioning that:

> The students can pronounce it skilfully and firmly, because they have already learned it from the previous Chinese lessons (Field Notes, 07/11/2017).

After the students completed their drama performances in Chinese for four rounds, they were instructed to sit in a circle on the floor. They were informed that:

> 'Now, we are going to do a matching activity. On the right side of the floor, the flashcards are the Chinese sentences. On the left side of the floor, the flashcards are the English translations. All of them have been distributed randomly on the floor. You are going to match the Chinese one with the corresponding English one.' At that time, Mingxu suddenly spoke out 'Oh, I know them — the meanings for them.' Other students also seemed confident about this activity (Field Notes, 07/11/2017).
>
> Ya'nan was selected to match the first sentence - 'nǐhǎo (你好), wǒ yào yī gè shòusī (我要一个寿司).' She didn't have any hesitation to choose 'Hello, can I have a Sushi Roll?' Then, Jìng Qí was invited to do the second one. When it came to 'hǎode (好的), sān yuán qián (3元钱),' she can pronounce it beautifully in Chinese. However, Jingqi was a little confused with the meaning of it, she initially tended to choose 'Here you are' for that Chinese sentence. While, at that

time Haoran immediately stopped her from doing that, advising her to pick up 'Sure, that would be 3 dollars.' Then, 'Do you agree with that?' I asked. 'Yes,' they said together. Jingqi also nodded her head to indicate her agreement and understanding of that sentence's meaning (Field Notes, 07/11/2017).

In terms of 'xièxie (谢谢) and zàijiàn(再见)':

'The left ones were much easier,' Zixuan said, whilst yelling out 'Me, me, me.' I then responded 'OK, please choose the meanings of xièxie (谢谢) for us.' Immediately, he picked up the flashcard with 'Thanks' self-assuredly (Field Notes, 07/11/2017).

During the whole process, the students were encouraged to use Chinese as much as they could, even though this was the first time they had encountered the Chinese sentence patterns — 'wǒ yào yī gè' (我要一个)··· and 'gěi nǐ qián' (给你钱). Obviously, 'Drama Performing' was very popular among the local students for learning Chinese, and they commented:

Yujia: I love it. I think it is really cool, because we get to think of the food that we have in the English menu, that is the other way to learn another language. Yi'na: People all have fun and a lot of learning at the same time.Yajing: I like doing the drama performances. Because we have fun, and we get to see the Chinese money, and we get to see how we get the...show the stuff in Chinese (Focus Group B, Year 4, 28/11/2017).

What is more, the classroom teachers shed light on their own positive and supportive attitudes and opinions towards such teaching strategies, which engaged the students in learning Chinese in a lifelike situation:

With the shopping, they like the role-play. It is not only the role-play, but because actually, they relate to them as you actually took the food we have from the canteen, and the menu from our canteen, and you used them in the lessons. You know, they can relate it to themselves. Otherwise, if they cannot relate the information no matter what it is, Chinese or English, they cannot relate it to themselves. They are not going to care much about it or learn much or be more engaged. So I think the lessons you had on the canteen and the food have been really successful (Classroom Teacher, Ms. Mu, Year 5, 21/11/2017).

Again it comes back to making connections. It is really a good strategy, because it allows them to connect their own real-life experiences with trying to remember or learn, and figure out what the new words or content is. That is really a strong way for them to make meaning of what you want them to learn (Classroom Teacher, Mr. Ke, Year 4, 28/11/2017).

As the above information indicates, teaching Chinese under the guidance of the concept 'huìshēnghuìsè' (绘声绘色) in the school-based context helps to construct such an authentic learning space for allowing spoken Chinese to occur naturally in the local students' real-life experiences. Based on this concept, the teaching focus was on how the above-mentioned learning activities were adopted to direct the teacher-researcher to utilise the tangible 'shēng – 声' (voice – the oral expressions) and the concrete 'sè – 色' (appearance/colour – the stuff) from the local students' daily school-based learning practices. Initially, in terms of 'shēng – 声' and 'sè – 色' they were linked to the 'Drama Performing,' which was intended to get the students to speak and use Chinese in their familiar context within the school-based community by means of utilising such shopping language and materials from their actual lives. This allowed the mutual construction of a 'miniature' authentic and localised situation for making Chinese happen habitually. Meanwhile, such an interactive activity acted out in Chinese class was also favoured by the local classroom teachers, who said:

What we have been focusing on at school as well in other learning areas is influencing, and learning to get messages from the situation, learning to get messages from the text that is not written (Classroom Teacher, Ms. Shen, Year 3, 07/12/2017).

Shopping in Chinese is quite effective because you link them to the things that were available in the canteen. The things they might be able to role play doing in the canteen. So it is relating to the things they actually do, putting them into their real context for them. And it is obvious when they go to the canteen they would be shopping and buying the things they need. They know how to buy

> things. It is an engaging activity. Also when you do the role to play it, so they role-play being the customer, or being the shop keeper, this is very engaging as well (Classroom Teacher, Ms. Shi, Year 4, 05/12/2017).

The strategy of 'Drama Performing' is also widely used by the local classroom teachers for teaching their students other subjects at school. And this teaching strategy and learning style has been accepted by and is attractive to both boys and girls. Accordingly, the pedagogical belief 'huìshēnghuìsè' (绘声绘色) serves as a bridge for the Chinese teacher-researcher to reach the local students' funds of knowledge from their concrete school-based lives. 'Drama Performing' was an exact embodiment of 'huìshēnghuìsè'(绘声绘色), as the local students engaged in and demonstrated the relevant shopping language in Chinese. Once again the concept of 'huìshēnghuìsè' (绘声绘色) has been used to find out more forms of the local students' funds of knowledge which have accumulated in the school-based community, making Chinese more learnable for them. In this sense, the local students' prior knowledge from their real shopping experiences at the school canteen supplements the source and embodiment of their funds of knowledge, especially gathered in the school-based community. Their funds of knowledge here are their prior knowledge in regard to the linguistic terms commonly occurring in such shopping activity, such as how to initiate and end the conversation between the seller and the buyer, as well as how to order the food. As the evidence shows, such students' funds of knowledge are beneficial for them in developing a better understanding of the corresponding Chinese expressions used for this sort of shopping practice, particularly the Chinese sentences' meanings. The features of the 'Drama Performing' technique, as employed commonly in second language classrooms, were exemplified by Winston (2014):

> Drama is essentially a multimodal form of pedagogy, offering different points of entry for students' interests to be engaged. Good language teachers already make use of visual aids, of animation, of sound, of the possibilities afforded by new technologies. Drama, too, offers visual and auditory signs for students to make sense of but the difference is that the multimodality of drama pedagogy largely depends upon the presence of live bodies (p.4).

When it comes to the benefits of adopting drama as a teaching scheme for language teachers, Winston also made the following points:

> One of the potential strengths of drama for language teachers is its social nature. Students being able and willing to work together, watch and listen to one another, talk through ideas and improvise together, shape material, and present it in groups — such is the very stuff of the drama classroom. The spirit that characterises such work at its best is that of the ensemble — where everyone supports everyone else for the benefit of the whole group. Such an atmosphere is necessarily founded on trust and co-operation and will, when achieved, encourage students to find their own voices, lose their inhibitions, contribute, and speak out in class (2014, p.5).

Based on the students' in-class engagement in the learning activity entitled 'You Draw, I Guess,' it was observed that:

> Very soon, the student started the first drawing based on the picture shown to him, which was 'ròubǐng (肉饼).' Then, another team member was thinking for a while, responding 'Sorry, I know what that is in English, but I forgot how to say that in Chinese.' Then, I asked other students in class 'Can you help her?' Simultaneously, they responded 'ròubǐng.' I replied 'It is correct, let us continue this game.' Then the boy continued his drawing after I showed him the flashcard 'shòusī (寿司).' As for this word, this girl made a quick response, saying 'shòusī' exactly. I said 'Well done.' Naturally, the last word was 'chǎofàn (炒饭).' The boy drew a simple bowl with some rice on top of it. That girl — Yujia was thinking for a second, answering 'chǎofàn.' Finally, this took them 2 minutes and 52 seconds (Field Notes, 14/11/2017).

The second group of students encountered a similar situation: the respondent forgot how to say 'fried rice' in Chinese. This took them 2 minutes and 30 seconds. The third group of students not only did a good job in drawing, but also presented a quick and exact reaction towards the pronunciations and meanings of the three food vocabularies. It is worth stating that when they came to the last vocabulary — 'ròubǐng,' even though the boy did not draw the

corresponding picture for 'ròu bǐng,' another student can speak out 'ròubǐng' quickly and confidently. That saved some time for this group. This took them 1 minute and 50 seconds (Field Notes, 14/11/2017).

Afterwards, students also revealed their affection for this sort of activity, which was adopted in class for the purpose of reinforcing their familiarity with the pronunciations and meanings of newly-learned Chinese vocabularies, as follows:

> Haoxuan: I think the drawing is fun, because I like drawing. And getting into learning and drawing at the same time is fun. Yi'na: We have a lot of fun doing it. And we all work together in turns to do it. And we enjoy drawing as well (Focus Group B, Year 4, 28/11/2017).

It turned out that the students really enjoyed this learning style in class, which helped them to more easily engage in learning such Chinese vocabularies through vivid drawing and mutual cooperation.

Another learning activity entitled 'Picking Mushrooms' was conducted in the following way. Firstly, the students were instructed to sit in a circle on the floor. Then, they were required to read the rules together loudly. Subsequently, an instruction and a demonstration were given to them, namely 'Please pick a hóngsè (红色) mushroom for nǐhǎo (你好), wǒ yào yī gè shòusī (我要一个寿司), then please quickly put a hóngsè (红色) mushroom beside that sentence.' It is worth stating that the foundation for this learning activity is not only the students' knowledge about the three newly-learned Chinese food vocabularies and those Chinese sentences. More importantly, the Chinese colour vocabularies are the very essence of supporting their completion of this learning activity. Thus, at the very beginning, the learned colour vocabularies were reviewed to make sure that they could still remember their pronunciations and meanings. To my delight, most of them were still able to pronounce them very well and be clear in their meanings. Next, after all the 'mushrooms' and flashcards with the Chinese sentences' pronunciations had been distributed randomly on the floor, the first instruction was given:

Please pick a 'zǐsè (紫色)' mushroom for 'zhè shì nǐ de shòusī (这是你的寿司).' Then, I asked 'Who wants to be the first one?' The first student — Tiān Yòu actively and highly raised his hand. Then, I chose him to answer this question. I saw that he could quickly pick up a purple mushroom. After he was thinking for a while, then he put it beside the sentence 'nǐhǎo (你好), wǒ yào yī gè shòusī (我要一个寿司).' Subsequently, I tentatively asked him 'are you sure of this choice?' He looked at me, nodding his head firmly to indicate his confirmation. After that, I asked other students that 'Do you agree with his choice?' They said 'No' together. Then, I repeated the sentence twice. Very quickly, Tianlei raised his hand, and was invited to make another choice. He told me that 'zhè shì nǐ de shòusī' means 'Here is your Sushi roll.' I said 'It is right'(Field Notes, 21/11/2017).

As for picking the second and the third mushrooms, I said:

Please pick a 'lǜsè (绿色)' mushroom for 'hǎode (好的), sān yuán qián (3元钱).' Mingxuan chose the right colour for such a Chinese sentence quickly. I responded to him 'Well done.' The following instruction was 'Please pick a lánsè (蓝色) mushroom for gěi nǐ qián (给你钱).' Then, I invited Ya'nan to choose one. When noticing her hesitation concerning that Chinese sentence, I repeated the sentence — 'gěi nǐ qián (给你钱).' Immediately, she made the right decision on it (Field Notes, 21/11/2017).

Upon noticing that the students were already familiar with this learning activity, I announced:

'Now, Mr. Zhao needs an assistant to give instructions like that in Chinese. Who is going to be the Chinese teacher now?' I asked. Then Meijing was invited to give instructions in Chinese and select students to answer her question. Subsequently, she said 'Please pick a hóngsè (红色) mushroom for zàijiàn (再见).' I responded towards her 'Sorry for that, Mr. Zhao lost the hóngsè (红色) mushroom.' So she said 'Please pick a báisè (白色) mushroom for zàijiàn (再见)' clearly, as well as invited Yu'na to do this. After finishing that correctly, Yu'na was advised to choose the more difficult one among the two Chinese sentences

> left, including 'xièxie (谢谢),' and 'nǐhǎo, wǒ yào yī gè shòusī (你好，我要一个寿司).' Hence, she gave the instruction 'Please pick a fěnsè (粉色) mushroom for nǐhǎo, wǒ yào yī gè shòusī (你好，我要一个寿司).' After that, the girl Jingxiang picked a 'huángsè (黄色)' mushroom for the last Chinese expression 'xiè xie (谢谢),' but she forgot how to say 'yellow' in Chinese. At that moment, their classroom teacher spoke to all the students that 'Everybody should know how to say yellow.' Then, they said 'huángsè (黄色)' together. Due to her mutual efforts with other classmates, Jingxiang did well (Field Notes, 21/11/2017).

After finishing reviewing the sentences, there were two different coloured mushrooms left, namely 'hēisè (黑色) and zōngsè (棕色).' However, there were three food vocabularies left. Therefore, I then encouraged them to pick one mushroom to representtwo food vocabularies at once. It was observed that:

> Yuxun gave an instruction 'pick a "hēisè (黑色)" mushroom, and then put it beside 'ròubǐng (肉饼),' together with 'chǎofàn (炒饭).' After hearing that, Jingyi completed it quickly and exactly (Field Notes, 21/11/2017).

As soon as they finished picking all the different coloured mushrooms for each Chinese sentence, the students were required to make a response towards the English meanings of such Chinese sentences. In doing so, it was noticed that:

> Even though the students were rather slow to respond to the English meanings, they can still provide exact feedback on understanding the English meanings of such Chinese sentences (Field Notes, 21/11/2017).

Therefore, through conducting this activity the students not only became familiar with the pronunciations and meanings of the learned three food vocabularies, as well as the corresponding Chinese sentences used for shopping at the school canteen. They also came to associate the learned Chinese colour vocabularies with such newly-learned Chinese knowledge.

Later on, a group of students expressed their fondness for the in-class activities employed for learning the relevant linguistic terms used for daily shopping at the school canteen:

> Yujia: I think the drama one that I learned more, because we got to learn new food and things in Chinese. So if we want to go to China, what I can do is to ask something for food. Ruxue: I like 'Picking Mushrooms' very well, because we also get to learn colours in that. And we also get to pick the colour mushrooms. So we can also get to learn (Focus Group A, Year 3, 07/12/2017).

Additionally, employing the concept 'huìshēnghuìsè' (绘声绘色) in designing and practising the learning activities, such as 'You Draw, I Guess' and 'Picking Mushrooms' assists the teacher-researcher to concentrate on the function of 'sè – 色' (appearance/colour) for engaging the local students in getting more familiar with the Chinese shopping language, through drawing on their existing knowledge concerning the colour vocabularies learned and retained from earlier Chinese lessons at school, as well as incorporating their preferred drawing activity. Originally, in Chinese 'sè – 色' means 'colour' without the help of any context in 'huìshēnghuìsè' (绘声绘色). Here, making use of the students' learned Chinese colour vocabularies sets up a vivid situation for employing Chinese in the representation of 'sè – 色'(colour vocabularies and the drawn images). Furthermore, one of the classroom teachers provided the following remarks in regard to such learning activities' contribution to the students' learning and use of the Chinese shopping language:

> I think it works quite well, because they should have been reasonably familiar with the colours, and the names because I record them, being told the colours in Chinese Year 1 and Year 2. So that should have been [their] 'existing knowledge' that has been sort of reactive activities. So hopefully, they would remember it. And when you go back to the previously learned words and stuff, it just helps to consolidate it for them (Classroom Teacher, Ms. Shi, Year 4, 05/12/2017).

Most of the students in this local public school have transferred some of their personal time to learn Chinese at school, even after school due to the support for Chinese learning from the local Department of Education. This modification to course arrangements gives the local students wider and more convenient access to learning Chinese in the school-based community. Large groupings of these students had been exposed to learning Chinese colour vocabularies in Year 1 and Year 2, and most of them have retained such knowledge. The Chinese teacher-researcher has activated such students' funds of knowledge (here especially referring to their existing knowledge concerning the learned Chinese colour vocabularies) to engage them in a 'knowledgeable' role in mastering the new Chinese knowledge — enhancing their shopping language and food vocabulary by the instruction of the 'sè – 色' (appearance/colour) from the concept of 'huìshēnghuìsè' (绘声绘色). Such knowledge is beneficial for enriching their familiarity with the newly-learned Chinese expressions used for shopping at the school canteen, conceivably establishing a genuine learning environment for their absorption of the localised Chinese language.

Following the above analysis, 'shēng – 声' (voice, the oral expressions), accompanied by 'sè – 色' (appearance/colour, the actual materials) jointly interacts in 'huìshēnghuìsè' (绘声绘色) during the process of teaching the Chinese linguistic terms in relation to shopping practice. This provides a channel for making spoken Chinese happen via a natural learning circumstance, based on being aware of the local students' different embodiments of their funds of knowledge (here meaning their prior knowledge and existing knowledge) that were attained in the school-based community. Meanwhile, the actual learning materials, such as the apron, the Chinese paper money, the updated Chinese menu, as well as the food flashcards, were essentially adopted for mobilising, and then utilising their valuable funds of knowledge, thus making "Chinese happen as part of the localised shopping activity in a real-life environment and reducing their unfamiliarity with the learning of Chinese in class.

9.5 Wùjìnqíyòng – 物尽“棋”(其)用[1], rénjìnqícái – 人尽“棋”(其)才[2]

The following lesson plan(Table 9.7) relates to teaching the linguistic terms which occurred in playing chess.

Table 9.7 Lesson plan for teaching linguistic terms used in playing chess

Term 3 & Week 3 — Week 8	**Unit Title: Playing Chess – xiàngqí – 象棋 (chess)**	**Date: 15/08/2017—19/09/2017**	**Class: Year 3 & Year 4**
Expected Learning Outcomes	Initially, students are expected to search the vocabularies, including ‘King,’ ‘Queen,’ ‘Knight,’ ‘Castle/Rook,’ ‘Bishop,’ and ‘Pawn’ through using the iPads in the form of working as a team, and then draw them on A3 paper with the corresponding Chinese pronunciations. Then, the students will be instructed to present their search results in Chinese through combining them with simple Chinese sentence patterns, such as ‘zhè shì – 这是’ (this is) and ‘nà shì – 那是 (that is).’ Afterwards, the activity entitled ‘Let’s Rap’will be adopted in order to help the students get more familiar with the sentence patterns, including ‘zhè shì – 这是’ (this is) and ‘nà shì – 那是 (that is),’ as well as the Chinese vocabularies concerning the pieces used in playing xiàngqí – 象棋 (chess). Subsequently, the devised game ‘Do What I Said’ will be employed to get the students familiar with the action words which occurred in playing chess, namely ‘hold’ (ná – 拿), as well as ‘move’ (yídòng – 移动). Finally, the popular game ‘Try Your Luck’ will be used as the assessment activity for evaluating the anticipated learning outcomes. Therefore, after learning such Chinese expressions related to playing xiàngqí – 象棋 (chess), the students are expected to be able to use these Chinese expressions when playing chess at school.		

1 The original source of the Chinese version: 马烽《典型事例》:“这倒是人尽其才，物尽其用，两全其美。” It refers to making the best use of everything available, such as materials or resources in order to get them to serve their proper purpose.

2 The original source of the Chinese version:《淮南子·兵略训》:“若乃人尽其才，悉用其力。” It means that everyone can do their best to complete some tasks or deal with some difficulties through fully utilising their own advantages and abilities.

Continued

Term 3 & Week 3 — Week 8	Unit Title: Playing Chess – xiàngqí – 象棋 (chess)	Date: 15/08/2017—19/09/2017	Class: Year 3 & Year 4
Lesson Outline	Class Learning Activities Class Evaluation Activity	Using iPads to Search the Chinese Pronunciations of Vocabularies regarding the Role Names of Chess Pieces: 1. Students will be instructed to work in a team with six or seven members based on their own decisions. 2. One student will be selected as the team leader to bring a pencil case and an iPad. 3. After all the preparatory work is done, the following instructions will be given by showing one picture with the vocabularies to be searched by their own including. 4. While the students are searching the vocabularies, they are encouraged to present their 'masterpieces' in the form of drawing these roles of chess pieces, as well as writing down the corresponding Chinese pīnyīn (拼音) and hànzì (汉字) on a pre-given A3 paper. Let's Rap: Yo, yo, dàjiā hǎo, wǒ de míngzi jiào... 哟，哟，大家好，我的名字叫 zhè shì qíshì hé hēixiàng. 这是骑士和黑象。 nà shì xiǎobīng hé báijū. 那是小兵和白车。 zhè shì guówáng hé wánghòu. 这是国王和王后。 wǒ ài xiàngqí, go, go, go! 我爱象棋，去，去，去! Yo, yo, hello, everybody, my name is... This is the knight and black bishop. That is the small pawn and white rook/castle. This is the king and queen. I like chess, go, go, go! Review Activity — 我 (I) 说 (Say) 什么 (What)，你 (You) 做 (Do) 什么 (What) – 'Please Do What I Said': 1. Six students work in a team. 2. The first round: Three students will give instructions in Chinese one by one by using the flashcards, and the other three students do what they heard from them one by one. 3. The second round: They swap the roles to complete the same task.	

Continued

Term 3 & Week 3 — Week 8	**Unit Title: Playing Chess – xiàngqí – 象棋 (chess)**	**Date: 15/08/2017—19/09/2017**	**Class: Year 3 & Year 4**
Lesson Outline	Class Learning Activities Class Evaluation Activity	Note: The team that spends the least time and does it correctly will be the winning group. Assessment Activity: 'Try Your Luck' 1. Four students work in a group. 2. Firstly, please tell Mr. Zhao on which side you want to try your luck. 3. According to the number on the dice you have got, you can choose the times you want to try in the chatterbox. 4. Please act out the action you have got from the chatterbox. Note: Please remember you need to say the number you got, as well as read and answer the question from the chatterbox in Chinese.	
Teacher's Role		The teacher's role will be as an instructor and a facilitator during the process of giving a lecture and conducting the class activities separately.	

Concerning the students' reaction towards the first learning activity, it was found that:

> One team had a fabulous drawing and labelling for these vocabularies. Each of them was responsible for each Chinese vocabulary that was searched and drawn. Two girls were a little shy in this group, however, one girl was extremely outgoing and active and could perform class activities very well, no matter whether she was alone or worked with other classmates in class. She was the team leader for this group who can create a very active and passionate learning environment for team members (Field Notes, 22/08/2017).

The students and their classroom teacher separately observed:

> Yajing: They helped us so we like finding out the meaning of the role of chess pieces, and we typed the Chinese chess pieces on a board and it told us how to say the names of the 'king,' 'queen,' and all the other ones. And I do know how to use [the] iPad. I have one. Yi'na: Yeah, [it helps]. Because we do not just get to learn [Chinese language] one way. We can like learning Chinese in different ways. You can just get them to learn from the iPads easily. And most kids know

how to use [the] iPad (Focus Group B, Year 4, 28/11/2017).

I think obviously it is very effective as well. The kids, they love using the technology, giving them that independence to kind of search for themselves what they want to do. It is an effective strategy (Classroom Teacher, Mr. Ke, Year 4, 28/11/2017).

Apparently, using advanced technology, especially portable digital learning devices, for instance iPads, intrinsically engages these students' learning of Chinese in class through allowing their own independent searching, drawing, and writing in the form of working as a team. Such autonomous learning styles for Chinese language teaching, are hugely popular among the local school students, as this gives them independence and they do diversified tasks. Given these students' various characteristics, it is stressed that in a knowledge-based society teachers should be aware of students' learning experiences from their own daily exposure to using digital tools for educational purposes, such as laptops or tablets inside and outside school (Lai, Khaddage & Knezek, 2013). It is better for teachers to differentiate their teaching pedagogies through linking such students' 'technology-enhanced informal learning experiences' (p.421) to their formal learning at school, thereby building a shared and inspired learning space in class (Lai, Khaddage & Knezek, 2013). Another technique this teacher-researcher employed was the use of 'rapping' to help the students memorise the learned Chinese sentences and vocabularies used for playing chess. Some vocabularies with certain rhymes were added to the end of each sentence, taking advantage of the possible similarities in pronunciations between Chinese and English. However, as to the activity entitled 'Let's Rap,' boys and girls indicated their different preferences in class.

Haoxuan is a little shy boy, while he is a very attentive student in any of my Chinese lessons. Sometimes, I preferred to ask him whether or not to participate in a class activity, he always shook his head, indicating his refusal to participate in it. Today, when I was asking him 'Do you like rapping?' he nodded happily and confidently, responding with 'Yes.' As it was his show time, Haoxuan walked to the front of the classroom confidently and calmly. He was completely absorbed in his performance, without any hesitation and shyness. At the end of his rapping performance, he even showed us an action just like a real rapper. More importantly, Haoxuan also demonstrated his fluent and fantastic pronunciation of the Chinese linguistic terms used in this rap (Field Notes, 29/08/2017).

Meanwhile, a quiet boy, Bochao from another class also revealed his great talent and interest in this rap activity. Compared with his previous participation in Chinese lessons, this time he did give me a deep impression of his amazing rapping expertise:

When being asked 'Who would like to be the first one to give us a demonstration?' Bochao was the first student to raise his hand quickly and actively in class. In my memory, this gentle boy was always sitting quietly at the back of his classmates in Chinese lessons, concentrating on the learning content. However, he was scarcely willing to take part in activities in front of other classmates. Previously, a similar activity was conducted to introduce the food and the colours that they liked. In that rap activity, Bochao was active and confident enough to show it in front of other classmates and teachers. No matter whether it was previously or today, that boy was trying his best to be a real rapper by using the learned Chinese expressions with the help of his preferred singing form — rap (Field Notes, 29/08/2017).

The teacher-researcher recalled other incidents from the particular day's teaching episodes in the following field notes:

Some girls just refused to attempt the rapping at the front of the classroom. Because some girls did not show much interest in this style of music, whereas many boys enjoyed the rapping activities. Even though initially many of the students were too shy to act it out in front of class, they would wave their hands and open their mouths to follow the students who were rapping (Field Notes, 29/08/2017).

Particularly among the girls, it was found that:

They preferred to rap with another partner/girl classmate in front. Namely, girls were more willing to complete this sort of activity in the form of team cooperation in order to overcome their anxiety and fear of performing rapping individually (Field Notes, 29/08/2017).

Conversely, during recess on campus, two boys informed me that:

> They really like rapping in their daily life, while showing me their body movements and gestures that commonly occur in a rapping performance, just like a real rapper. The two boys also indicated their intention to be involved in such a kind of activity again in class (Field Notes, 29/08/2017).

Furthermore, the students voiced their own ideas concerning the rapping activity used for learning such Chinese linguistic terms:

> Haoxuan: I like doing the rapping, because it is fun and we got to learn in groups. Yi'na: I am not really a big fan of doing it. But then watching people doing it is fun (Focus Group B, Year 4, 28/11/2017).
>
> Yujia: More boys like it, in my opinion. But I think both genders can do it because I only do see many girls rapping, so I think more girls should try, give them a try. Ya'nan: I think I learn a lot because I am listening to some Chinese raps and I understand that. Because sometimes I might want to know how to rap in English, then I can rap in another language. Ruxue: I like it because we get to learn like we understand the language to different languages and we get to rap. So what they can rap like we can rap different English songs, rap in Chinese. My favourite rapper is DJ Kelly (Focus Group A, Year 3, 07/12/2017).

Rapping as a learning activity to engage male and female pupils in learning Chinese in the Australian local classroom encountered different reactions, such as active participation, enjoyable appreciation, and a neutral attitude. Clearly, different styles of singing and musical encounters resulted in various classroom interactions, sometimes according to gender. Classroom engagement and disengagement happened differently between individuals, small same-sex groups, and within the larger grouping of genders.

Currently, the more popular genre of choice is 'hip hop,' and young students are having great fun with it. Its popularity is strengthened when it is performed as a rap, which has a very strong cadence and lyrics which have good repetitive language features. Nevertheless, it was noticed that this kind of musical form which created a leaner 'buy-in' mostly attracted the boys, and only a small number of girls were willing to be involved in the rapping activities in class. Historically speaking, the musical genre of hip hop is traditionally dominated by male rappers, which originally reflects that it is rooted in African-American culture, particularly the younger generations (Mohammed-baksh & Callison, 2015). This teacher-researcher had to be careful that when using this style of Rap music in teaching Chinese, he did create disengagement as a result of using a popular music style which historically sits within a strong male gender orientation.

At the same time, the teacher-researcher's conversations with their classroom teachers with regard to the integration of rapping in Chinese language teaching reflected that:

> Yeah, the rapping is great. Some of them may be too shy to do that, but they still would like to watch the others get up and do it. So I really enjoyed watching that. As for fun, it is even to say, you know, in China, there are eastern rappers, they say what it sounds like to them, they compare it to their own, western rappers. So [that is] engaging them (Classroom Teacher, Ms. Mu, Year 5, 21/11/2017).
>
> It is very engaging, especially for the boys who are very interested in that activity. And music is really a fun way to get the children to remember that vocabulary. They really know well when they are singing, and they enjoy that, too. So again doing something that is fun and doing something helps them learn the vocabulary we can repeat lots of, lots of that kind of thing. Later on, we can use it in the classroom every day to practice (Classroom Teacher, Ms. Shen, Year 3, 07/12/2017).

According to the classroom teachers' feedback, even after class utilising rapping as a teaching strategy can effectively involve the students in the learning content through the cadent rhythm characterised by hip hop music. By doing so, the local students can also immerse themselves in a familiar cultural style as a language carrier for attaining Chinese knowledge in an entertaining and stress-free way. The actual benefits of employing rapping to another completely novel learning domain

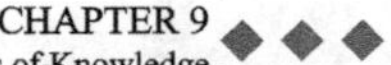

far outweigh its drawbacks. Such a phenomenon was also noticed by a classroom teacher in Chinese class, who said that:

> It just helps connect their own interest and their own modern-day culture. And to connect with something new helps them retain the information, the world's language a lot better. I guess it comes down to they are probably learning without realising they are learning, because they just think they are having fun. But actually, when they go back the next week, they can remember all the stuff you were doing in the rap, because 'Oh, I did not realise absorbing this, I just have fun with the microphone around,' actually said some kids (Classroom Teacher, Mr. Ke, Year 4, 28/11/2017).

It also has been noted by Hanan (2014) that hip hop, for the purpose of educational use, can potentially increase students' academic achievements through deploying their multi-faceted intelligences, for example, body movements which match the attractive beat. Meanwhile, it is widely favoured by the youth, because such a musical style assists the students who are otherwise confronted by trying to express tunes accurately, who can now 'sing' in a casual and relaxing manner (Hanan, 2014). Crucially, rapping allows young students to more easily build up their self-assurance and lessen their anxiety via constructing a socially-appropriate and expressively-encouraging atmosphere in class (Segal, 2014). Another activity, entitled 'Do What I Said' was developed to help the students review the vocabularies which occurred in playing xiàngqí (象棋). Before conducting this activity, one student, Zixuan who is the language expert in Chinese class, was invited to work with the Chinese teacher-researcher, demonstrating how to complete this activity in the form of a team. Students were required to choose team members (around six students in a group) quickly. In the first round, three students gave instructions in Chinese one by one via using the flashcards. The other three students enacted what they heard from their team members one by one. In the second round, they were required to swap roles to complete the same task. Meanwhile, they were informed that the team that spent the least time and did it correctly would be the winning group. Because of the different students' characteristics in different groups, both expected and unexpected learning outcomes were observed in this activity:

The first group was made up of six boys. They completed the task almost exactly, based on the designated rules for this activity. They practiced the pronunciations and meanings of 'ná (拿) for hold' and 'yídòng (移动) for move,' as well as the names of qízǐ – 棋子 (chess pieces) in xiàngqí – 象棋 (chess) without my assistance or others' help. The students in this group tended to think on their own or had minor discussions with team members, even though when they were not sure of which 'qízǐ' they needed to 'ná' or 'yídòng,' namely in Chinese it is described as 'jǔqíbùdìng – 举棋不定' (Field Notes, 12/09/2017).

As for the second team, they were more willing to negotiate with others in a group to make the right or exact decision before they spoke them out in Chinese. As Zixuan is a 'Chinese language expert' in this class, he can pronounce the vocabularies on the flashcards quickly and precisely, as well as get the exact meanings of them. In this group, he really set a good example for other students, playing a role as a team leader (Field Notes, 12/09/2017).

It is worth noting that Zixuan always liked to instruct other students to complete this learning task well. This phenomenon also occurred with Haoyu today, a boy from the first group, when it was noticed that:

When the girls in the third group were conducting this activity, Haoyu said that 'the girls did not speak these words out in Chinese, they just put the qízǐ – 棋子 (chess pieces) on the top of each flashcard.' At once, he showed these girls how to do this activity while saying the Chinese vocabularies in his mouth fluently and correctly. Then, the girls' team knew how to complete this activity and did it again (Field Notes, 12/09/2017).

After class, some of the students provided the following feedback and their views on this learning activity:

Haoxuan: I like working in a group, because when I am working with my friends, if you get stumped they can help you out. Yi'na: The same [with Haoxuan]. And also you and your friends can like learning together and have fun (Focus Group B, Year 4, 28/11/2017).

Their classroom teacher then informed the teacher-researcher of the following information:

> It allows them to support each other, particularly in our class there are kids who are more advanced, becoming experts, and having those students be able to work with other students. It quite advances, allows them to share their knowledge really ... yeah become expert learners (Classroom Teacher, Mr. Ke, Year 4, 28/11/2017).

On the whole, when the students were instructed to perform such class learning activities that needed their joint efforts, they were always more active and did it much better than when they worked individually. Namely, the power of a team's cooperation is always stronger than that of the individual, due to the encouragement and positive influences from their peers, as well as the power of role models.

As for the assessment activity, a well-known game 'Try Your Luck' was used in the form of the chatterbox to help the students recall the knowledge learned from the previous Chinese lessons, ranging from the learned Chinese numbers, and colours, to the vocabularies concerning playing chess. To play this game, the students were directed to work as a team. Two dice with numbers were prepared to meet the different ability levels of the students. Most of them can say the numbers from 1 to 10 in Chinese, while a few of them can even speak them out from 0 to 30. Subsequently, once the chatterbox was opened, they would see four different colours inside and requirements on the back/opposite side which they were required to complete. The students from the first group did a very good demonstration for the other teams. This group's students performed this activity completely, according to the rules shown to them on the screen, which are described as follows:

> The students selected the dice with numbers from 1 to 12, which means they were likely to speak out some numbers beyond 10 in Chinese. That undoubtedly added a little bit of difficulty for this group in this game. Finally, they got the number '12.' Beyond my expectation, they can speak out 'shí (10) ... shí (10) ... èr (2) ... èr (2) ...' simultaneously, which impressed me deeply. Afterwards, they chose 'lǜsè – 绿色' (green), and got the instruction —'qǐng

ná guówáng – 请拿国王' (Please hold the king). Then, one student acted out this corresponding action by using the prepared qízǐ – 棋子 (chess pieces) on the qípán – 棋盘 (chess board) (Field Notes, 19/09/2017).

The classroom teacher later made these comments:

> It was once again, a game where they don't realise that they are being assessed. So that's quite good for you to see whether or not they can, what they have retained, what they can do. Obviously, once they had made a little chatterbox, and then used the colours in Chinese, you know, whatever the words, you can see whether or not people have that, or you can see who supports each other. But they are really engaging, because it is a game (Classroom Teacher, Ms. Shi, Year 4, 19/09/2017).

Being a gender inclusive game-based learning task, by its very nature, the above-mentioned activities attracted most students' attention and were entertaining learning styles and experiences for them. Research has shown that real game-based learning activities help learners to easily concentrate on the gaming content in relation to English expressions, especially when interacting with advanced learners during the process of playing games (Ryu, 2013). Here, various chess gaming-related learning activities were constructed and applied to the Chinese language classroom for the purpose of cultivating the local students' Chinese linguistic awareness and familiarity with these necessary expressions which occurred in playing chess. Gradually, the local students became capable of using such Chinese words, verb phrases, or simple sentences while engaging in this recurrent gaming practice with their peers, who are both experts at playing chess and learning Chinese in the school-based community, thereby boosting their daily usage of Chinese and advancing their Chinese speaking abilities.

Therefore, the data, in the form of observations, showed the local students' learning experiences, as well as the students' opinions and their classroom teachers' perspectives concerning teaching the linguistic terms which frequently occurred in playing chess. Targeting the tangible learning content and effective teaching happenings, for instance, as measured by the metaphor 'wùjìnqíyòng – 物尽棋(其)

用, rénjìnqícái – 人尽棋(其)才' is required to make full use of the local conditions, especially the materials and resources in the school-based community, as well as to thoroughly exploit the local students' aptitudes for the purpose of making Chinese a local and learnable language. In terms of the concept of 'wùjìnqíyòng – 物尽棋(其)用, rénjìnqícái – 人尽棋(其)才' engendered from the data illustrations, the school-engaged program helped the Chinese teacher-researcher to build a school-based intellectual community, blending the learning resources available in school, as well as the local students' various forms of knowledge retained from their daily learning into making the localised and student-centred teaching plans for Chinese language learning.

As for 'wùjìnqíyòng,' the authorised written form is '物尽其用,' instead of '物尽棋用.' While they share the same pronunciation, they function as a pun. Here, the first aspect of 'wùjìnqíyòng – 物尽棋用,' is manifested in the convenient access to the chess-based gaming gadgets in the school campus and classroom for these local students, where they can easily expose themselves to using chess pieces and chess boards during their school time. As for the second aspect of 'wùjìnqíyòng – 物尽其用,' it specifically refers to completely utilising such digital learning tools, including iPads, laptops or computers that are well-resourced in each classroom in this local public school. In this sense, the technology-based knowledge co-construction focuses on triggering, recruiting, and applying the handy learning tools in school for the local students' learning of Chinese through the collaboration-based learning form. To be exact, each classroom in this school is equipped with a certain number of iPads, laptops, or computers for the students to learn and have fun at the same time. Furthermore, the receivers and kits used for connecting wireless are available in each classroom. That is to say, having easy access to these learning devices and this equipment in school facilitates the student-students' collaborative learning of Chinese happening on a regular basis. Recognising these 'wù – 物' (things) from this local public school, including the chess playing resources and the digital educational instruments, drove the Chinese teacher-researcher to incorporate these reachable learning resources into Chinese language teaching, thus enabling their potentially valuable 'yòng – 用' (applications) to be thoroughly activated and appropriately served for making Chinese a local and learnable language.

Another applicable Chinese metaphor is 'rénjìnqícái – 人尽棋(其)才,' and the original written form for 'qí cái' in 'rénjìnqícái' is '其才.' Here, firstly using 'qí cái - 棋才' (knowledge/skills about playing chess), rather than 'qí cái – 其才' (wit/talents in different fields) suggests that the local students already have abundant information concerning how to play chess, as they play it at school. In particular, this sort of students' universal knowledge formed in the school-based community in regard to properly playing chess shares the characteristic of gender inclusiveness, hence neutralising the impact of the sex differences that exclusive knowledge can engender. At this point, the students' general knowledge about playing chess has become part of their firm and positive prior knowledge that was retained from the previously interactive learning process within the school-based setting.

Another role of 'rénjìnqícái – 人尽棋(其)才' lies in '其才' (wit/talents in different fields), in preference to 'qí cái – 棋才' (knowledge/skills on playing chess). For example, having the students in class utilise iPads, laptops, or computers, and their preferred drawing activity as their independent learning tools, is effective in generating a vocabulary inventory regarding chess gaming. This learning process depends heavily on pooling their wisdom regarding the use of advanced technology and art designing talent. Encouraging their collaborative learning takes advantage of the students' communal intellectual repertoires, including their powerful knowledge of using that advanced digital learning equipment, as well as their prior knowledge of sketching skills, correspondingly minimising the side effects caused by individual learning in an unfamiliar subject.

Likewise, with the introduction of rap into learning Chinese, an additional manifestation of the local students' powerful knowledge was identified, namely their rapping endowments and competencies, as a significant discovery of a different form of their funds of knowledge. As noted by Roth and Erstad (2013), the art genre related to hip-hop music is deeply rooted in young people's community-based lives, being embodied as their funds of knowledge and cultural traits. Furthermore, it is stressed that adopting students' interest-based knowledge is conducive to developing their inclusive powerful knowledge in a holistic way, as they are equipped with the opportunities for becoming 'experts' within their acquainted domains (Maton, 2014; Kinchin, 2016). This type of students' funds of knowledge (here referred to as their powerful knowledge of rapping) takes on some gender variances, as rap is appreciated mostly by male students. In this study, even though most of the girls in class were reluctant to perform rap individually, they tended to be involved in it through peer-to-peer alliances or by enjoying watching other students' rapping performances.

Finally, the integration of the paper game entitled 'Try Your Luck,' using a chatterbox to enhance the students' learning of the linguistic terms used in playing chess, is also deeply reflected in the metaphor 'wùjìnqíyòng – 物尽棋(其)用, rénjìnqícái – 人尽棋(其)才' through their two reciprocal dimensions. On the one hand, when it comes to 'wù – 物,' the chatterbox is a game gadget made simply of sheets of paper at hand. On the other hand, reflecting the concept of 'qí yòng – 棋(其)用,' inside the chatterbox are relevant, carefully prepared questions, aimed at assisting the students to go through the learnt Chinese expressions concerning playing chess. Following 'wùjìnqíyòng – 物尽棋(其)用, rénjìnqícái – 人尽棋(其)才' articulates the local students' intellectual contributions regarding not only knowing how to make and play a chatterbox game, but also keeping the learned Chinese number and colour vocabularies in mind. Tapping into such inclusive students' funds of knowledge produced in the school-based community, such as making and playing a chatterbox game (their prior knowledge), as well as knowing the Chinese number and colour vocabularies (their existing knowledge) can both help them to reach their optimal learning outcomes in regard to the Chinese linguistic terms used for playing chess.

These metaphors 'wùjìnqíyòng – 物尽棋(其)用,'and 'rénjìnqícái – 人尽棋(其)才' suggest that searching the local students' intellectual storage can allow the Chinese teacher-researcher to retrieve the multi-layered embodiments of their funds of knowledge, here particularly referring to their powerful knowledge of using advanced technology and rapping expertise, their prior knowledge of drawing and playing the paper-made game — chatterbox, together with their existing knowledge of the learned Chinese vocabularies concerning the numbers and the colours. Therefore, realising all the mentioned forms of the local students' intellectual repertoires helps to create and maintain a well-developed relationship for knowledge co-construction between the Chinese teacher-researcher and the local students in the school-based community.

9.6 Students' Funds of Knowledge-Oriented Instruction Strategies

As indicated by the aforementioned, employing the instruction strategies in combination with the local students' diverse knowledge bases, such as their prior knowledge, existing knowledge, and powerful knowledge, will reinforce engagement and learning efficacy in Chinese class. The corresponding knowledge foundation is established and consolidated during the process of interacting with their peers in the local school-based community. The concept of students' 'funds of knowledge' focuses on their home-based 'perspectives and methods of inquiry that led to that knowledge' (González et al., 2005, p.19). In this regard, through the process of interacting with the local school students' learning of Chinese, the teacher-researcher gradually finds that the local students are not agents who passively receive the information, as they learn different subjects at school. Actually, they possess their own preferences in choice-making about learning content and activities to suit their diverse learning levels and abilities at school. Consequently, the class learning activities are designed and carried out from the perspective of being pupil-directed and self-initiated. The well-resourced learning activities are built on the local students' available funds of knowledge, which they have picked up and retained from their daily school experiences. To utilise the knowledge formed in the school-based milieu as much as possible requires the Chinese teacher-researcher to work as an 'enabler' and a 'sensor,' to furnish the students with discourse power in terms of deciding on their suitable and preferred learning tasks and activities in Chinese class. Furthermore, when it comes to the advantages of employing such popular class learning activities, a group of students mentioned:

> Ya'nan: I like it [Minion Says], because we got to learn it in English, then we get to learn it in Chinese. Yujia: I like drawing, because when we get to draw we can also learn at the same time, like we did this [drawing] one (Focus Group A, Year 3, 07/12/2017).

At the same time, classroom teachers expressed their own opinions regarding such diverse interactive activities adopted in Chinese class, which engendered multi-layered values in terms of students' engagement and learning achievements as follows:

> Yeah, for lots of them, they like to, you know, sketch down their ideas, it can be creative. So I think that is engaging, so once we were talking more, getting them to write, and getting them to create can be really beneficial. It allows them to be proud of their own work. For them, they do reflect upon their work. And then for you to assess them, you know, in that whole group's area which is the only time you get real access (Classroom Teacher, Ms. Mu, Year 5, 21/11/2017).
>
> So they really enjoy a variety of activities. It really needs a variety [of activities]. It cannot be just the same thing over and over. But when we use things, like drawing, the games they really enjoy. That increases learning. They learn better in that way (Classroom Teacher, Ms. Shen, Year 3, 07/12/2017).

Characteristically, all the above-mentioned learning activities and instruction styles utilised for engaging the local students in learning Chinese share the joint feature that they abound with resourceful and available funds of knowledge obtained during their school time, including their prior knowledge, existing knowledge and powerful knowledge, which are presented in different styles. That is to say, the various forms of their funds of knowledge are mostly relevant to and accumulated from their previous learning experiences in the school-based community, such as knowledge concerning acting out 'minion says,' playing the 'charades' game, 'drawing & designing' works, doing role-play activities and singing the English birthday song (their prior knowledge), knowledge regarding the formerly-learned Chinese language for the number and colour words (their existing knowledge), as well as knowledge on utilising advanced technology and performing hip hop music (their powerful knowledge).

Through mobilising and deploying such knowledge, some students emerge as the language 'experts' in this school-based learning community. Initially, that is visibly reflected in the situated learning practices, such as the sporting-related, shopping-related, and chess gaming-related role-play activities. It is not surprising to observe that these 'expert pupils' are willing to use their learned Chinese language knowledge to help and encourage their peers who have difficulty or who are shy in engaging with learning Chinese in class. Such a phenomenon implies that the 'peer demonstration' or 'class model' should be encouraged and exploited as a positive influence on these students' attainments of novel Chinese language knowledge. Such

situatedness creates the essential condition and resource for achieving a student-centred Chinese curriculum construction via symbolising the legitimate peripheral participation In this school-based community of practice (Lave & Wenger, 1991). To be exact, through participating in such situated learning activities, the students tend to reshape their original identities (from being silent bystanders to active participants) in this real learning community of Chinese language practices. Being the 'legitimate members' in such a Chinese learning community also helps to reduce their inner tension and conflict, as these students naturally involve themselves in interactions with their peers, friends, and classmates through being exposed to their joint social practices, rather than being restricted to individual learning exercises.

Employing teaching tactics, such as art-oriented, music-based, action-oriented, and technology-related collaborative activities effectively triggers the local students' potential bilingual identities (shifting between the English domain and Chinese sphere) for effecting their translanguaging aptitudes which were developed in the Chinese classroom. Such a situation reflects a Chinese metaphor, namely the local students are well 'shēntǐlìxíng – 身体力行' (earnestly practising and experiencing what has been learned), they're already obtained different forms of knowledge in a flexible and sustainable manner in Chinese class. García and Wei (2014) argued that 'translanguaging enables emergent bilinguals to enter into a text that is encoded through language practices with which they're not quite familiar' and 'to truly show what they know' (p.80). Grounded in the current research context, the utilisation of learners' translanguaging capabilities is here linked and committed to making (spoken) Chinese a localised and learnable language for Australian students through exploring their various embodiments of funds of knowledge shaped in the school-based community. In this sense, the significance of adopting such learning activities in Chinese class on the one hand lies in constructing a real situation-based learning space where the students are able to retrieve their prior, existing, and powerful knowledge for mobilising their translanguaging competencies. On the other hand, this real learning community for implementing their localised social practices positions the local students into a tangible place and space for making Chinese (L2) happen in the form of various local practices through mediating their L1 knowledge (English). In this way, this deepens our understanding of the notion of translanguaging (Creese & Blackledge, 2010; García & Wei, 2014) and 'language as a local practice' (Pennycook, 2010), and broadens its practical application to the field of Chinese language education.

Employing multidimensional student-centred instruction strategies contributes to facilitating the emergence of these students' dynamic bilingualism through activating their potential translanguaging capabilities in Chinese class. Meanwhile, these contextualised learning activities are attached as important to the sustainable learning of Chinese from the ecological perspective. Progressively, such a tangible Chinese learning community in school tends to develop into a place where the local students are encouraged to study as a team for knowledge co-production, thereby enabling the 'pupil-directed translanguaging' to happen naturally through their being continually exposed to self-regulated language learning practices and their retained knowledge (García, 2009; Lewis, Jones & Baker, 2012b; García & Wei, 2014). The turn to such bilingual pedagogy mainly concentrates on utilising the local students' already established knowledge base to make connections for their absorbption of new information. Comparatively, such student-centred learning activities are not only very popular among the local school students in terms of making Chinese learnable for them, but also stimulate the natural occurrence of learner-directed translanguaging in the Chinese classroom. Therefore, integrating these multi-faceted students' funds of knowledge-oriented instruction strategies into such localised learning content can mutually make Chinese a learnable language for tAustralian local school students.

9.7 Conclusion

This section illustrated and analysed the Chinese teacher-researcher's practical teaching experiences, incorporating the concepts of 'xǐwénlèjiàn – 喜闻乐见' 'lǎnglǎngshàngkǒu – 朗朗上口,' 'rónghuìguàntōng – 融会贯通,' 'huìshēnghuìsè –绘声绘色,' and 'wùjìnqíyòng – 物尽棋(其)用, rénjìnqícái – 人尽棋(其)才' into learning the sports activities-based content, celebratory song-based content, mathematical calculation-based content, canteen shopping-based content, chess playing-based content separately. Collectively, the teaching practices based on these students' interests identified the local students' diverse embodiments of their funds of knowledge that were shaped and preserved within the school-based community, which are manifested in three forms, namely their prior knowledge, their existing knowledge, as well as their powerful knowledge. Meanwhile, such pedagogical strategies derived from the corresponding Chinese metaphors altered the teaching pattern from the teacher-directed style to the mode of student-focused and peer-peer collaboration-based knowledge co-construction. This harmonious confluence helped the native Chinese teacher-researcher to establish an authentic and interactive learning space and place in which the local students were endowed with rewarding conditions for nurturing their emergent bilinguals as translanguaging abilities, by virtue of experiencing those situated learning practices in Chinese class.

CHAPTER 10

Students' Sociolinguistic Activities-Based and Funds of Knowledge-Oriented Curriculum Construction for Making Chinese Learnable

This study explored the potential educational uses of the local students' English language expressions as they occurred in their daily recurring sociolinguistic activities in the school-based community to select curriculum content and develop pedagogies for English-to-Chinese transfer to improve the learnability of the Chinese language. The primary focus has been on whether and how such content sources from the local students' daily recurring sociolinguistic activities have engaged them in learning Chinese and made speaking Chinese part of their everyday practices through mobilising their funds of knowledge concerning curriculum co-construction. To justify such focus, the local students' discourse power has been empowered in terms of selecting their preferred and proper learning content and teaching activities, thus identifying their more intellectual and linguistic repertoires that contribute to making Chinese a localised and learnable language for them.

This research project first depicted the five forms of the local students' daily recurring sociolinguistic activities that they perform in English at school by observing, categorising, and conceptualising them during the process of conducting teaching of the Chinese language in this local public school. Based on such findings, the English linguistic terms that frequently occurred in these activities were elicited by way of these students' mutual discussions in class. They jointly selected and constructed the potentially suitable learning content for the Chinese language on their own. This endeavour, as shown in Chapter 8, re-developed the original concept of 'language as a local practice' (Pennycook, 2010). To be precise, investigating the embodiments of the local students' daily practices that frequently happened in the school-based community enriched this concept in the process of developing Chinese language education. This was in preference to verifying and theorising such everyday regular sociolinguistic activities that can encourage the speaking of Chinese as a localised and learnable language. What became subsequently significant in this study was to provide an analysis in Chapter 9, concerning how to make such Chinese learning content reach its optimal effect on students' learning outcomes. Accordingly, to present the learning content in a widely understandable and preferable manner and style, the teacher-researcher combined it with relevant instructional strategies partly derived from indigenous Chinese metaphors for mobilising their knowledge base shaped in the school-based community, thereby extending the notion of 'funds of knowledge' (González et al., 2005) to the field of Chinese language education. In doing so, different students' features from dissimilar educational backgrounds and places should be taken into consideration and addressed during the process of adapting and adopting such Australian localised learning materials.

The empirical findings and theoretical influences of this investigation itself will be elucidated in depth in the subsequent section. The teacher-researcher has demonstrated the analysis of the evidence collected from his Chinese teaching experiences through appropriately employing such Chinese metaphors as 'liàngtǐcáiyī' (量体裁衣), 'jiùdìqǔcái' (就地取材) and 'zhǔrénwēng yìshí' (主人翁意识) for improving on Pennycook's (2010) statement concerning 'language as a local practice,' as well as through enacting these students' funds of knowledge formed within the school-based community based on González and others' concept (2005) of the children's 'funds of knowledge' learned through participation in household-based community practices. The teacher-researcher intended to pursue and validate a foundation for his arguments through analysing and theorising about the local students' daily recurring sociolinguistic activities and their funds of knowledge at school, as well as such corresponding Chinese learning content sources and instruction strategies jointly constructed among the students in class. That is to say, the teacher-researcher was particularly keen to use instructive tactics deriving from those Chinese metaphors. Such Chinese concepts were of value in guiding the teacher-researcher to effectively conduct the Chinese lessons for the local school children, as well as identify the intellectual treasures hidden within them. In this regard, the localised learning resources, together with the student-centred teaching strategies reciprocally made Chinese learnable, as the local students' potential to translanguage between English language and the Chinese language (Canagarajah, 2011; García & Wei, 2014) became powerful through participating in the situated Chinese learning practices in the school-based community (Lave & Wenger, 1991). Informed by the evidence from the students' and their classroom teachers' feedback, the localised learning content and appropriate instruction approaches had multi-faceted influences on these students' learning achievements in the Chinese language in this Australian local public school. This also led to further analysis regarding how to make these learning resources and relevant teaching activities generated from this local school comprehensively available and helpful for other learners of Chinese from wider communities. Then, a corresponding prerequisite for utilising such Australian localised learning materials for Chinese language education globally was proposed: they should be adjusted according to Chinese learners' educational and cultural backgrounds.

To mobilise that wider and profound appropriateness and influence for such learners, the function of 'yīndìzhìyí (因地制宜)[1]' was accordingly reflected through the following evidence excerpts:

> I think definitely these activities would be definitely translated. I think they could enjoy that well. I think they would work. They are valuable and important for the children to learn another language. That helps them communicate effectively with others. And that helps them learn more about their own language as well. And doing it this way, using the information they already have, and

1 The original source of the Chinese version: 汉·赵晔《吴越春秋·阖闾内传》:"夫筑城郭，立仓库，因地制宜，岂有天气之数以威邻国者乎？" Originally, it means taking suitable measures or making reasonable decisions to deal with something should be based on the local specific conditions, especially as they occurred and applied in the field of agriculture.

learning about the things they use in their everyday life. It is very valuable and important. Or the activities could be modified. If at different schools, they did not play basketball, but they played soccer, you could use the same sort of ideas that you use for soccer, football, cricket, or something else, adapt in that way to suit each class, each school (Classroom Teacher, Ms. Shen, Year 3, 07/12/2017).

I would say most of what you have done would slip into Canadian, or American schools quite well. It is not particularly Australian. If you did and got some Australian animals, I think you can do a little bit of Australian animals, you would tweak it there. You would make it Canadian animals — moose, you know, beaver. Or American you might have different animals there. You would tweak that slightly to relate it more towards what the students know there. I am pretty sure in America they sing 'Happy Birthday' the same as us. And they may not have acanteen, but they would have a ... cafeteria. But I think the majority of those lessons would slip into the Canadian or American classrooms with little difficulty, so they would be very suitable for students in Canada or America. And I think the fact ... because they are beginners, it is the beginning phase. The information is very basic. And everybody needs to say basic information to start off (Classroom Teacher, Ms. Shi, Year 4, 05/12/2017).

The two local classroom teachers were aware that the learning content and teaching activities adopted for the Australian local school students' learning of Chinese were very effective in engaging them and suitable for their learning interests and levels. However, when being further asked about the usefulness and worth of such learning materials for other learners of Chinese from different regions of the world, they both tended to express a similar viewpoint — 'yīndìzhìyí (因地制宜).' When it comes to the topic in relation to sporting activities, including handball, ping pong, and basketball, this was particularly relevant to the Australian Chinese language classroom, whereas in different countries their native ball sports, such as football or cricket can be adapted and re-used to suit those students' interests and needs in learning Chinese there.

Similarly, the other classroom teacher's suggestion that different learning topics, such as animals or school shopping should concentrate on the typical and actual phenomena that exist in those particular areas. At the same time, she held a positive and supportive attitude that the learning resources offered to her students in the Australian local school-based setting would be also valuable for other learners of Chinese around the world, such as American or Canadian pupils. That is because such learning material is very fundamental in achieving communicative purposes for beginning learners of Chinese, no matter whether in Australia or in other parts of the world. Furthermore, the idea of 'yīndìzhìyí (因地制宜)' was identified and demonstrated in another two perspectives:

> I guess that they would be [suitable] for the same age group. Because what you are doing is ... if you were trying to engage Canadians or Americans, I think because you definitely make the activities related to them. So everything you do from the canteen, or the games they play. I think they would be suitable for those kids of the same age as them. But I am not sure. I guess so (Classroom Teacher, Ms. Mu, Year 5, 21/11/2017).
>
> I think any ... any kind of similar school systems, like America, even England. These different types of strategies have been shown to work with these types of learners. I know a lot of Asian countries use different styles of teaching, but these kinds of activities are creative. I think they will be very effective in similar schools since they learn about these. It works very well for those students in terms of their learning the content. I think that would be very effective (Classroom Teacher, Mr. Ke, Year 4, 28/11/2017).

Obviously, the pre-condition for reaching the optimal outcomes from the localised Chinese learning content and teaching activities is that learners need to be from similar age groupings, as well as comparable schooling environments. When applying such Australian localised Chinese learning content to other learners from diverse educational backgrounds, it is necessary to be alert to the real age of these 'actors' and the actual 'places' where learning and use of Chinese are likely to happen. Given these two essential elements, the potential value and efficacy of such localised Chinese learning resources can be activated to a certain extent in order to exactly satisfy similar learners' desires in learning Chinese. For example, because of the cultural differences between Western countries and Asian countries, such student-centred teaching strategies may not be suitable for emergent second-language learners of Chinese in the Asian school-based setting, which is likely to result in conflicts between dissimilar teaching beliefs and learning styles. That means such localised learning resources produced for enriching and sustaining children's learning of Chinese are rooted in the Australian in-built sociocultural traits.

Nevertheless, the current learning material provided online for overseas learners of Chinese is confronted with the urgent issue of lacking 'authenticity, appropriateness and affordability' (p.41) as highlighted by Erbaggio et al. (2016), thus failing to engage various learners who have the desire to choose Chinese as their second/foreign language. Here, the concept of 'yīndìzhìyí (因地制宜)' helps to mobilise the potential learnability and suitability of such localised learning materials shaped in this Australian school-based community for other learners of Chinese from wider communities around the world. The importance of 'yīndìzhìyí (因地制宜)' guides other teachers of Chinese who would like to transfer and utilise those localised learning resources to take their students' specific characteristics and existing realities from different educational traditions into consideration. In this case, the flow and exchange of these obtainable and suitable Chinese learning materials would be effected flexibly and perceived as adaptable in an intellectual hybrid space which caters to more exterior actors' (other emergent second language learners of Chinese) keenness and need to share and gain access to the handy and valuable Chinese learning resources.

The findings accordingly pointed out the prospect and condition for mobilising the suitability of such learning materials produced within an Australian school-based community for other learners of Chinese from manifold areas around the world. Figure 10.1 displays the interactive and interconnected relationship between the elements which are central to this study, the figure is used as the evolving trajectory for theorising the localised and student-centred curriculum construction of Chinese language learning in this book.

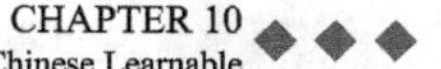

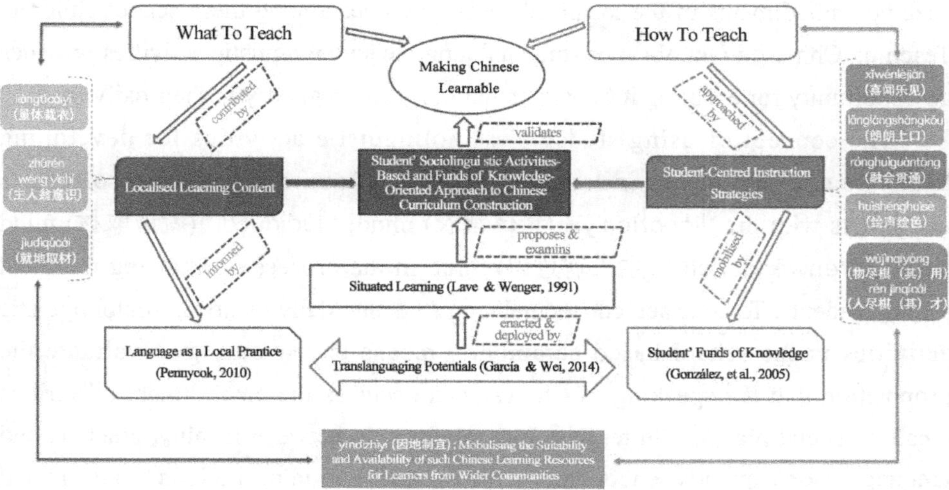

Figure 10.1 The developmental trajectory of this study

Therefore, the above-mentioned research discoveries have been applied to explore the learnable content sources and effective instruction strategies for constructing a localised and student-centred Chinese language curriculum, an approach which is formulated as the students' sociolinguistic activities-based and funds of knowledge-oriented curriculum construction for the learning of Chinese.

10.1 Conceptualising Students' Sociolinguistic Activities and Funds of Knowledge for Learning of Chinese Language

This section offers a discussion of the fundamental components to add to the notion of students' sociolinguistic activities and funds of knowledge for the learning of Chinese, given the necessity to elucidate the relationship between the localised social practices and the students' funds of knowledge shaped in the school-based community. It is worth exploring the local students' daily recurring sociolinguistic activities for the purpose of constructing a localised and learnable curriculum for their learning of Chinese. The various forms of the local students' daily sociolinguistic activities which recur in the school-based community are the specific embodiments of the localised social practices among these school children. Teaching Chinese in the form of students' tangible sociolinguistic activities provides an opportunity for enabling it to happen naturally and regularly in their daily lives.

The concept of using students' sociolinguistic activities for developing learnable content sources in learning Chinese reflects this teacher-researcher's encounters with the 'liàngtǐcáiyī' (量体裁衣) mind, 'jiùdìqǔcái' (就地取材) mind and 'zhǔrénwēng yìshí' (主人翁意识) mind in the process of knowing the local school students. To be exact, conceptualising students' daily recurring sociolinguistic activities in the school-based community means endeavouring to validate the proposition that the speaking of Chinese can occur as the embodiment of various localised social practices in terms of the relationship between locality, practice, and language. Consequently, encounters with the above guiding notions would reveal the interrelationships among them, thereby embodying the process in regard to how Chinese can be made a localised language through enacting such social practices in the school-based community. The natures of 'locality' and 'practice' are particularly exemplified through the process of 'jiùdìqǔcái' (就地取材), which mainly suggests that handy resources in this local public school can be exploited as assisted learning tools for Chinese teaching. Based on the teacher-researcher's daily observations, different types of balls for sporting activities are provided in this school, such as handballs, pingpong balls, and basketballs. The corresponding sporting fields and equipment are well-prepared on campus for these children to play with during recess. Likewise, it was noticed that there is an abundance of instruments used for the students' chess gaming, both in the playground and in the classroom. Also, the internet is available in each classroom, along with electronic and multimedia teaching and learning devices, such as iPads, laptops, desktops, and projectors for these students to retrieve and master their desired knowledge quickly and efficiently. Accordingly, during the school time, the students' frequent use of such resourceful materials to perform their corresponding activities while speaking English symbolise the very essence of 'locality' and 'practice' from the perspective of the notion of 'jiùdìqǔcái' (就地取材). That is to say, the popular sporting practices in this local school, including playing handball, pingpong, and basketball are regularly enacted by these students via their daily repeated exposure to such sports-related equipment.

The traditional practice of chess is played on a regular basis, no matter whether they are learning to play it properly for a competition, or just doing it for fun at school. Birthday celebrations, mathematical calculations, and canteen shopping are characterised by recurrent practices in this local school-based community. Given the above-mentioned, the internal link between 'locality' and 'practice' is reflected by two of its purposes. One is to make use of the existing educational resources within this local school. The other is to discover the multi-faceted forms of these local students' daily recurring activities, performed in English, as the students involve themselves in employing such chess and sporting-related equipment and participate in other habitual practices at school. These two constituents are mutually labelled as 'locality' and 'practice' for teaching Chinese in the local context, thus localising Chinese language education from the angle of constructing such localised learning content in the school-based community.

Following 'jiùdìqǔcái' (就地取材), 'liàngtǐcáiyī' (量体裁衣) is another concept employed, during the process of knowing the local students, by the Chineseteacher-researcher to appropriately apply these potentially educational resources and intellectual treasures with 'locality' and 'practice' to teaching the local children Chinese in the school-based community. As the original meaning of 'liàngtǐcáiyī' (量体裁衣) suggests, when utilising such localised learning materials from students' daily recurring sociolinguistic activities in this school-related context, the appropriateness and learnability of such resources should be considered in terms of these students' ages, cultural and educational backgrounds, previous learning experiences of Chinese, as well as their capacities for receiving and mastering new information. As a whole, the notion of 'liàngtǐcáiyī' (量体裁衣), accompanied by 'jiùdìqǔcái' (就地取材) jointly specifies and shapes the 'locality' and 'practice' for learning and using Chinese in such a tangible localised context. As 'jiùdìqǔcái' (就地取材) and 'liàngtǐcáiyī' (量体裁衣)mutually interact with 'locality' and 'practice,' they produce the perception of 'zhǔrénwēng yìshí' (主人翁意识) with regard to utilising these valuable resources from that 'practice' with such 'locality' to construct a localised curriculum for Chinese language learning, being focused on these local students' interests and characteristics in the school-based context. Hence, in considering the 'liàngtǐcáiyī' (量体裁衣) mind, 'jiùdìqǔcái' (就地取材)

mind and 'zhǔrénwēng yìshí' (主人翁意识) mind in the process of knowing the local students, the three components reciprocally facilitate the use of Chinese in such familiar environments from the school-based community, namely making Chinese an embodiment of students' daily recurring school-based social practices. Such a process of completing second language socialisation (SLS) has been described as:

> It does not look at language or development in a social vacuum, but sees it as inextricably linked with issues connected with identity, community (a sense of belonging), ideologies, and tensions of structure and agency. That is, unlike traditional SLA studies that focused principally on aspects of linguistic development and the increasing sophistication of a learner's proficiency, social approaches examine the relationships (or indexicality) between linguistic forms and practices, on the one hand, and the learner's social world, on the other, and also how those practices position the learner, and how identity is enacted in interaction (Duff & Doherty, 2018, p.86).

Clearly, school is seen as a miniature society wherein students play a role as 'actors' inborn with diverse personalities, such as being active, being passive, being smart and quick, or even being slow. However, they do shoulder correspondingly different kinds of 'tasks and responsibilities.' Here, teachers or educators undertake the role of a 'director' or a 'facilitator' to be carefully aware of these actors' various 'performances,' which are put on based on their own preferences and capabilities during daily school life. Such 'acts' are imbued with intellectual and linguistic resources for localising and socialising Chinese in the Australian context. That is to say, the school-based community is an ideal place for the Chinese teacher-researcher to explore these local pupils' actual linguistic expressions, as are frequently used in their recurrent practices within the structure of the local school, thereby authorising these 'actors' to 'draft' such 'actable scripts' on their own.

Therefore, with the help and support of the three interrelated concepts from the Chinese metaphors, Chinese as a second/foreign language for these local students has experienced its socialisation through being exposed to those situated language learning practices in Chinese class. This also entails that the concept of utilising sociolinguistic activities for constructing learnable Chinese materials is aimed at

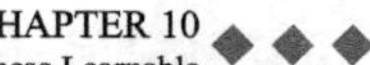

becoming deeply aware of the local students' learning styles and habits, as well as their own ideas on the expected Chinese learning tasks and activities, thus being conducive to enabling their agency and building positive identity in the learning of Chinese. Attributable to the enacting of Chinese as a foreign/second language through employing such authentic content sources from these local students' daily recurring sociolinguistic activities in the school-based community, their bilingual identity and communicative ability in learning and using Chinese have been built and enhanced to a certain extent.

Subsequently, the verification of the proposition of 'utilising students' funds of knowledge through participating in daily learning practices within the school-based community' aims to activate the local students' different forms of funds of knowledge accumulated in the school-based community. With such a starting point, what the local students can anticipate to achieve from Chinese class in terms of the learnable content would go beyond that which is abstractly suggested by the Australian K-10 Chinese Syllabus (2003) in non-localised settings. The local students' diverse forms of funds of knowledge reserved in the school-based community tend to easily engage them in learning Chinese, to enable the speaking of Chinese to happen in their familiar sociolinguistic activities and learning experiences.

A conceptualisation of the sociolinguistic activities and funds of knowledge utilised for generating the localised and student-centred learning content sources for Chinese language education can be considered with respect to their contributions to deploying the local students' emergent translanguaging abilities (Creese & Blackledge, 2010; Canagarajah, 2011; García & Wei, 2014) in Chinese class. In this regard, sociolinguistic activities can be regarded as an 'agent,' articulating a process of knowing the local students' linguistic repertoires to exert potential impacts on the construction of the learnable content of Chinese. This leads to the localisation of curriculum construction for the learning of Chinese. At the same time, the local students' funds of knowledge are formed and reserved by engaging in their daily learning practices within the school-based community. Considering that, the current Chinese syllabus and curriculum for Australian school students are ignorant of the significance of these students' hidden intellectual treasures. In shifting the attention from the teacher-directed approach to the student-focused approach during the process of conducting Chinese language teaching, opportunities for better understanding the local students' daily school lives and their learning styles emerge. In terms of the evidence analysed from the teaching practices, the roles of students' sociolinguistic activities and funds of knowledge are crucial in generating such localised learning content and student-centred instruction strategies, thus facilitating the emergence and application of the local school students' translanguaging propensities to make Chinese learnable for them.

Another question to be addressed in conceptualising students' sociolinguistic activities and funds of knowledge employed for developing the localised and student-centred learning materials for Chinese language education is: can the local students be provided with learning opportunities to express their own ideas on constructing the favoured learning content and activities in learning Chinese? In other words, do Chinese language educators or Chinese curriculum designers tend to create a space where Chinese learners with different characteristics can equally and actively share their thoughts on selecting the appropriate Chinese learning resources? In that case, the notion that sociolinguistic activities and funds of knowledge mutually create the conditions by which these young Chinese learners can establish their agency, thus offering them an opportunity of speaking for themselves in making Chinese learnable.

The concept of sociolinguistic activities in promoting the development of Chinese language education is accompanied by making the use of pupils' diverse funds of knowledge in the school-based community, especially for constructing the localised, learnable, and appropriate content sources for those overseas Chinese learners who have divergent learning backgrounds. Therefore, the curriculum construction of Chinese language learning needs to be slightly adjusted to meet the different and specific educational conditions for learners in other parts of the world.

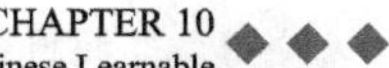

10.2 Students' Sociolinguistic Activities-Based and Funds of Knowledge-Oriented Approach for Constructing Localised, Student-Centred Chinese Curriculum

This research has proposed a students' sociolinguistic activities-based and funds of knowledge-oriented approach to construct a localised and student-centred curriculum for making Chinese learnable, that refrains from the 'one-dimensional' style that neglects different learners' features and needs in learning Chinese. Such a student-centred curriculum construction for learning Chinese recognises and adopts students' sociolinguistic activities and funds of knowledge to identify and employ localised content sources for teaching Chinese in diverse educational settings around the world. It also investigates and utilises students' funds of knowledge established and consolidated in the school-based community, enriching their engagement in discussing, screening, and producing suitable Chinese instruction resources and considering any contextual discrepancies.

Directed by a process of sociolinguistic activities-based and funds of knowledge-oriented curriculum construction, the internal attributes of knowledge co-production for learning of Chinese lie in two dimensions: one is being 'self-directed' (output from students), and the other is being 'self-enacted' (input by students), which are expected to be transferred to wider communities for benefiting overseas Chinese learners in different places in the world. In the case of teaching Chinese to Australian school students participating in the ROSETE Program, this study has probed into the local students' five daily recurring sociolinguistic activities at a public school in Western Sydney in NSW (Chapter 8). That allowed these students' diverse forms of localised social practices from the school-based community to be activated for effecting the situated learning of Chinese in the local classroom, thus potentially contributing to making Chinese learnable from the perspective of producing the localised learning content for them. Furthermore, the corresponding Chinese teaching practices deliberately employed the student-centred and learner-directed instruction strategies and styles that have been deeply rooted into the local students' learning habits during their schooling, such as 'xǐwénlèjiàn' (喜闻乐见), 'lǎnglǎngshàngkǒu' (朗朗上口), 'rónghuìguàntōng' (融会贯通), 'huìshēnghuìsè'

(绘声绘色) and ‘wùjìnqíyòng, rénjìnqícái’ [物尽棋(其)用,人尽棋(其)才] to better their engagement in learning such localised content in class.

In terms of making Chinese learnable, a prospective localised and student-centred curriculum construction tends to be implemented from two dimensions. The beginning dimension is the exploration of the local students’ daily sociolinguistic activities frequently performed in English at school; to be precise, identifying and making use of those recurring and common English linguistic terms uttered during such local students’ daily practices, for generating the appropriate Chinese learning content. The second dimension focuses on how to enhance the local students’ engagement in mastering the co-produced content through adopting their preferred teaching strategies and learning styles; that is to say, finding ways to make such localised Chinese learning content merge into these students’ real-life experiences, as their potential translanguaging competencies are stimulated in class. In this way, interweaving the above two elements, namely ‘what to teach’ and ‘how to teach,’ helped the beginning native Chinese teacher-researcher in his very initial stage towards striving for shaping a culturally appropriate and content-learnable curriculum based on the local students’ daily recurring sociolinguistic activities and funds of knowledge within the school-based community. However, students’ daily sociolinguistic activities and funds of knowledge can vary from place to place, embodying a range of regional and cultural differences to a certain extent. When applying the tactic of students’ sociolinguistic activities and funds of knowledge to wider learning communities for Chinese curriculum construction, the very natures of ‘locality’ and ‘practice’ need to be carefully considered when producing properly localised and student-centred Chinese learning materials.

The pedagogical concepts in relation to ‘localisation’ and ‘student-centredness’ are essential for constructing the students’ sociolinguistic activities-based and funds of knowledge-oriented curriculum for learning Chinese in different educational contexts worldwide. Specifically speaking, the student-centred notion here encompasses knowing the school students’ daily sociolinguistic activities for generating the localised learning content, as well as enacting their prior knowledge, existing knowledge, and powerful knowledge accumulated from different fields as their school-based funds of knowledge for employing the pupil-directed instruction strategies, alternatively offering another direction from which to better know the diversified characteristics among the potential Chinese learners. The purpose is hence to make various students' hidden linguistic and intellectual treasures 'surface above the water' and give them sound priority through generating the localised learning content, as well as employing the learner-focused teaching approaches. Therefore, the application and development of the student-centred pedagogy in Chinese language education is not only confined to generating students' learnable materials, but also focus on discovering their preferred instruction styles in the local educational environment during the process of interacting with their learning of Chinese in class. By doing so, the local students' evolving bilingualisms as their powerful translanguaging skills are stimulated, which in turn is conducive to building and shaping their positive identities and attitudes towards enriching their learning of Chinese.

Given the aforementioned, to make Chinese learnable for emergent second language learners of Chinese in other parts of the world, a principal mission is that Chinese teachers and educators, as well as policy makers, should be devoted to looking at the students' daily sociolinguistic activities and various funds of knowledge accumulated in different sociocultural contexts, which would have the potential to be developed into localised and student-centred Chinese learning materials and instruction approaches. The teacher-researcher in this case study has access to teaching Chinese to students who are studying in this Australian local public school. That provides an opportunity for pooling such intellectual and linguistic resources available in this school-based community to generate localised learning content and properly student-centred instruction methods for curriculum construction of Chinese language, ultimately making Chinese learnable for the Australian local school students. The students' daily recurring sociolinguistic activities-based and funds of knowledge-oriented curriculum construction is an essential constituent in terms of minimising the Australian school students' sense of unfamiliarity with the Chinese language in the local context. This can enhance their learning of and opportunities to use Chinese, as they perform their daily recurring social practices and learning activities in the school-based community, thus making Chinese a localised and learnable language for them. However, the model of utilising and constructing a students' sociolinguistic activities-based and funds of knowledge-oriented curriculum for Chinese language education has been proposed only for this one, single site case study in an Australian local public school. It would therefore be necessary to further examine and improve it to determine its applicability and practicality for transfer to the wider Chinese learning communities around the world.

10.3 Limitations and Recommendations for Future Research

The time for data collection was less than one year as per the restrictions of the ethical application process and the teaching period, which has limited the sample size of the data. Meanwhile, in terms of the major sources of data, the teacher-researcher's fieldwork journals were triangulated with the feedback from the students and the interviews wi–h their classroom teachers, but this can be done more extensively in future research. Here, it is worth mentioning that an alternative approach - a video elicitation interview is recommended, especially among younger participants, as that can better capture the dynamic moments of their recalling what had happened during the holistic process of learning Chinese in a vivid manner. This would elicit more unexpected and interesting information that would contribute to research findings, under the condition of being approved with the necessary ethical documents.

Furthermore, the research outcomes were narrowly sourced, not the 'measurable' evidence of knowledge acquisition, only coming from the specific learning environment and achievements in this school within the particular teaching period, as well as with the limited class numbers and a range of participants. Dissimilar teaching and learning contexts, as well as participants, may produce different results. The language repertoires of the children in the case study school were not ascertained, namely their linguistic diversity was not taken into account. Therefore, further research can be designed and carried out to engage more learners from a wider variety of learning communities locally and internationally, paying extra heed to their language repertoires, which may yield and verify other aspects that are influential on Chinese mastery.

More importantly, due to the teacher-researcher's own lack of in-depth professional knowledge, and limited teaching experience in Australian schools, this study was deficient in systematised curriculum design on language acquisition in terms of achieving the sequenced linking of vocabulary over each school term, across each Year level. Significant limitations were identified and acknowledged here including (a) linking structures were not provided, to enable complete simple utterances in Chinese; (b) although there was great vocabulary acquired, there were so few useful structures which were transferable; and (c) there were no linguistic connections between the activities in order to create intellectual mastery. Therefore, there is a great need for further research to generate follow-up evidence of sustained interest and mastery, and depart from the bigger perspective of Chinese language education in Australia based on 'Quality Teaching Framework' (DET, 2003). Under the direction of QTF, three key elements, including 'Intellectual Quality, Quality Learning Environment, and Significance' (DET, 2003, p.9) were recognised as a basis for future research to reflect a lack of professional knowledge of common language education practices in Australian schools.

10.4 Theoretical and Practical Contributions and Implications of this Study

This study has investigated the local students' daily recurring sociolinguistic activities and funds of knowledge in the school-based community that were utilised as the content sources for constructing a localised and student-centred curriculum of Chinese language learning within the Australian educational milieu. In doing so, the current research project provides some implications from the perspective of being theoretical and practical, which are illustrated as follows.

Initially, this research extended the notion of 'language as a local practice' (Pennycook, 2010) based on the proposition and understanding concerning how to make spoken Chinese the embodiment of the localised social practices through exploring the students' everyday recurring sociolinguistic activities in a local public school. Following that, those regular social practices which occurred in this school-based community were believed to abound with suitable content sources for constructing a localised and learnable Chinese curriculum. In this regard, to further conceptualise how the daily recurring sociolinguistic activities can be developed into potential Chinese learning content, indigenous Chinese metaphors were encountered, such as 'liàngtǐcáiyī' (量体裁衣), 'jiùdìqǔcái' (就地取材) and 'zhǔrénwēng yìshí' (主人翁意识) during the process of knowing 'what to teach.' In this way, the 'locality' and 'practice' (Pennycook, 2010) can be fulfilled by means of mobilising the local students' agency in terms of negotiating, selecting, and constructing their own preferred Chinese learning content in class. Such Chinese concepts helped the teacher-researcher to enable the local students' discourse power in a democratic and dialogic class structure. By doing so, these collected students' recurrent sociolinguistic activities performed in English in the school-based community were conducive to producing the localised Chinese learning content. Based on that, it was proposed that Chinese can be the embodiment of various local practices, which is an effective approach for constructing a localised curriculum for making Chinese learnable in the Australian educational environment. Previous work has mostly focused on applying the sociolinguistic activities to the field of teaching English as a foreign/second language, particularly through engaging in adults' daily social practices from the real world. This study formulated a novel approach, to bring in the students' (children's) daily recurring sociolinguistic activities in school for Chinese language education. In practice, this offers some insights for the native speaking Chinese teachers and educators, as well as for policy makers and Chinese syllabus makers, in also making Chinese learnable for diverse emergent second language learners of Chinese around the world.

At the same time, this study took a new look at students' funds of knowledge accumulated in the school-based community by way of deepening and re-developing the original concept of González and others (2005). In doing so, it was positioned in the context of teaching Chinese to Australian students through activating and deploying their various forms of funds of knowledge shaped in this local school-based community, which contributed to the generation of their preferred instruction strategies for constructing a student-centred Chinese curriculum. Being guided by indigenous Chinese metaphors with pedagogical meanings, such as 'xǐwénlèjiàn'

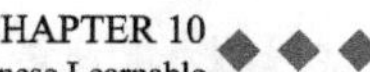

(喜闻乐见), 'lǎnglǎngshàngkǒu' (朗朗上口), 'rónghuìguàntōng' (融会贯通), 'huìshēnghuìsè' (绘声绘色) and 'wùjìnqíyòng, rénjìnqícái' [物尽棋(其)用,人尽棋(其)才], this research further identified three major students' knowledge categories, formed and preserved from their daily exposures to the learning experiences which happened in the school-based community, including their prior knowledge of those popular learning activities, existing knowledge of the formerly-learned Chinese language knowledge, as well as their powerful knowledge on using the advanced technology and rapping skills. Taking this into consideration, the current research project not only widened the notion and domain of 'funds of knowledge' (González et al., 2005) through engaging in those Chinese metaphors, but also supplied practical guidelines for teaching Chinese as a foreign/second language to those emergent language learners, especially employing inclusive and learner-directed teaching strategies. In this regard, this study proposed students' funds of knowledge-oriented instruction strategies in terms of how to teach Chinese to Australian local school students, with the adoption of their preferred teaching styles and learning habits in mind. Such an approach attempts to incorporate the students' favoured and habituated instruction manners and tactics into the student-centred Chinese curriculum construction, eventually making Chinese a localised and learnable language for them within the local educational milieu.

Afterwards, seeing the feedback from the local students' learning performance and outcomes in class and after class, the learning content from their daily recurring sociolinguistic activities, and the instruction strategies from their various shapes of funds of knowledge accumulated in the school-based community, mutually facilitated the students' 'translanguaging proficiency' to occur as their 'emergent bilinguals' (Creese & Blackledge, 2010; Canagarajah, 2011; García & Wei, 2014) for building their encouraging attitude and positive identity, and enriching their learning of Chinese within the local education context. The learning content from their localised social practices, along with their familiarised teaching approaches, was collectively beneficial for creating the situated learning practices (Lave & Wenger, 1991), making Chinese language teaching happen in a real, dialogic space in class, where they were allowed to put what had been learnt into practice, and for regular retrieval and authentic use, and gradually capturing fresh Chinese knowledge. Here, it is worth mentioning that the notion and practical application of translanguaging were extended to the field of teaching Chinese as a foreign/second language to Australian school students. Such a concept was further elucidated and embodied through the process of interacting with the local students' Chinese learning practices, as well as cultivating and theorising the localised and student-centred Chinese curriculum construction.

Accordingly, these localised and effective Chinese learning materials produced from such a real learning community tend to be transferred and dispensed to more emergent second language learners of Chinese from wider learning communities around the world with the support of advanced technology, such as the digital media and electronic learning devices, in a virtual, dialogic learning space. However, it was pointed out that such Australian localised Chinese learning resources need to be modified to suit Chinese learners with diversified cultural and educational backgrounds. The notion of 'yīndìzhìyí' (因地制宜) should be given the priority regarding mobilising its suitability for learners from wider communities.

In summary, this research project is significant in two main respects. On the one hand, it deconstructed, synthesised, and then reconstructed the discursive concepts that can be applied to the field of Chinese language education, based on the teacher-researcher's evolving translanguaging capabilities in terms of theorising the localised and student-centred curriculum construction for enriching the learnability of Chinese. On the other hand, this study informs the native speaking Chinese teachers and educators, as well as Chinese curriculum designers, concerning selecting and deciding what to teach, and how to teach, the emergent second language learners of Chinese when considering their diverse learning needs and educational characteristics from different places around the world, thereby making Chinese learnable for them.

References

Abrams, Z., & Schiestl, S. B. (2017). Using authentic materials to teach varieties of German: Reflections on a pedagogical experiment. *Die Unterrichtspraxis/Teaching German, 50*(2), 136-150. doi: https://doi.org/10.1111/tger.12038

Ahmed, S. (2017). Authentic ELT materials in the language classroom: An overview. *Journal of Applied Linguistics and Language Research, 4*(2), 181-202. Retrieved from www.jallr.com

AITSL. (2012). *Australian Professional Standards for Teachers*. Melbourne: Australian Institute for Teaching and School Leadership.

Alabsi, T. A. (2016). The effectiveness of role play strategy in teaching vocabulary. *Theory and Practice in Language Studies, 6*(2), 227-234. doi: http://dx.doi.org/10.17507/tpls.0602.02

Allehyani, B., Burnapp, D., & Wilson, J. (2017). A comparison of teaching materials (school textbooks vs authentic materials) from the perspective of English teachers and educational supervisors in Saudi Arabia. *International Journal of English Language and Linguistics Research, 5*(2), 1-14. Retrieved from http://www.eajournals.org/wp-content/uploads/A-Comparison-of-Teaching-Materials-School-Textbooks-Vs-Authentic-Materials-From-the-Perspective-of-English-Teachers-and-Educational-Supervisors-in-Saudi-Arabia.pdf

Altinyelken, H. (2011). Student-centred pedagogy in Turkey: Conceptualisations, interpretations and practices. *Journal of Education Policy, 26*(2), 137-160. doi: 10.1080/02680939.2010.504886

Australian Curriculum, Assessment and Reporting Authority (ACARA). (2013).

Australian Curriculum: Languages Chinese (revised). Retrieved from http://docs.acara.edu.au/resources/F-10_Australian_Curriculum_Languages_-_revised_Chinese_-_Nov_2013.pdf

Bailey, N. (2015). Attaining content and language integrated learning (CLIL) in the primary school classroom. *American Journal of Educational Research, 3*(4), 418-426. doi:10.12691/education-3-4-6

Board of Studies, Teaching and Educational Standards (BOSTES) NSW. (2003). *Chinese K-10 Syllabus*. Retrieved from https://www.boardofstudies.nsw.edu.au/syllabus_sc/pdf_doc/chinese_k10_syllabus.pdf

Butler, J. (2011). Using standardized tests to assess institution-wide student engagement. In R. Miller, E. Amsel, B. Kowalewski, B. Beins, K. Keith & B. Peden (Eds.), *Promoting Student Engagement Volume 1: Programs, Techniques and Opportunities* (pp.258-264). Syracuse, NY: Society for the Teaching of Psychology.

Baker, C. (2011). *Foundations of Bilingual Education and Bilingualism* (5th ed.). Buffalo, N.Y.: Multilingual Matters.

Barnawi, O. Z. (2009). The construction of identity in L2 academic classroom community: A small scale study of two Saudi MA in TESOL students at North American University. *Journal of Language and Linguistic Studies*, *5*(2), 62-84. Retrieved from http://www.jlls.org/index.php/jlls/article/view/82/82

Bransford, J. D., Brown, A. L., & Cocking, R. R. (2000). *How people learn: Brain, mind, experience, and school*. Washington, D.C.: National Academy Press.

Canagarajah, S. (2011). Codemeshing in academic writing: Identifying teachable strategies of translanguaging. *The Modern Language Journal*, *95*(3), 401-417. doi: 10.1111/j.1540-4781.2011.01207.x

Candlin, C. (1992). Preface. In D. Griffee (Ed.), *Songs in Action: Classroom Techniques and Resources* (pp.ix-x). New York: Prentice Hall.

Carter, S. (2006). Redefining literacy as a social practice. *Journal of Basic Writing, 25*(2), 94-125. Retrieved from https://www.jstor.org/stable/43443829

Castillo Losada, C. A., Insuasty, E. A., & Jaime Osorio, M. F. (2017). The impact of authentic materials and tasks on students' communicative competence at a Colombian language school. *Profile Issues in Teachers' Professional*

Development, 19(1), 89-104. doi: http://dx.doi.org/10.15446/profile.v19n1.56763

Chen, S., & Zhang, Y. (2014). Chinese language teaching in Australia. In X. L. Curdt-Christiansen & A. Hancock (Eds.), *Learning Chinese in Diasporic Communities: Many Pathways to Being Chinese* (pp.181-200). Amsterdam/Philadelphia: John Benjamins Publishing Company.

Chen, Z., & Yeung, A. (2015). Self-efficacy in teaching Chinese as a foreign language in Australian schools. *Australian Journal of Teacher Education*, *40*(8), 23-42. doi: 10.14221/ajte.2015v40n8.2

Cheng, M. T., She, H. C., & Annetta, L. A. (2015). Game immersion experience: Its hierarchical structure and impact on game-based science learning. *Journal of Computer Assisted Learning, 31*(3), 232-253.

Clarke, S. N., Howley, I., Resnick, L., & Rosé, C. P. (2016). Student agency to participate in dialogic science discussions. *Learning, Culture and Social Interaction, 10*, 27-39.

Cohen, L., Manion, L., & Morrison, K. (2011). *Research Methods in Education* (7th ed.). New York: Routledge.

Coles-Ritchie, M., & Charles, W. (2011). Indigenizing assessment using community funds of knowledge: A critical action research study. *Journal of American Indian Education, 50* (3), 26-41. Retrieved from https://www.jstor.org/stable/43608611

Coyle, D. (2013). Listening to learners: An investigation into 'successful learning' across CLIL contexts. *International Journal of Bilingual Education and Bilingualism, 16*(3), 244-266. doi: 10.1080/13670050.2013.777384

Crawford, J. (2012). *Aligning Your Curriculum to the Common Core State Standards.* Thousand Oaks, CA: Corwin Press.

Creese, A., & Blackledge, A. (2010). Translanguaging in the bilingual classroom: A pedagogy for learning and teaching?. *The Modern Language Journal*, *94*(1), 103-115. doi: 10.1111/j.1540-4781.2009.00986.x

Creese, A., & Blackledge, A. (2011). Ideologies and interactions in multilingual education: What can an ecological approach tell us about bilingual pedagogy?. In C. Hélot & M. Ó. Laoire (Eds.), *Language Policy for the*

Multilingual Classroom: Pedagogy of the Possible (pp.3-21). Buffalo, NY: Multilingual Matters.

Cummins, J. (2007). Rethinking monolingual instructional strategies in multilingual classroom. *The Canadian Journal of Applied Linguistics*, *10*(2), 221-240. Retrieved from https://journals.lib.unb.ca/index.php/CJAL/article/view/19743/21429

Dang, T. C. T., & Seals, C. (2018). An evaluation of primary English textbooks in Vietnam: A sociolinguistic perspective. *TESOL Journal*, *9*(1), 93-113. doi: 10.1002/tesj.309

Department of Education and Training (DET). (2003). *Quality teaching in NSW public schools: Discussion paper*. Sydney: State of NSW Department of Education and Training Professional Support and Curriculum Directorate.

Diao, W. (2016). Gender, youth and authenticity: Peer Mandarin socialization among American students in a Chinese college dorm. In R. A. van Compernolle & J. McGregor (Eds.), *Authenticity, Language and Interaction in Second Language Contexts* (pp.109-130). Bristol: Channel View Publications.

Ditchburn, G. M. (2012). The Australian curriculum: Finding the hidden narrative?. *Critical Studies in Education, 53*(3), 347-360. doi: 10.1080/17508487.2012.703137

Dobao, A. F. (2016). Peer interaction and learning. In M. Sato & S. Ballinger (Eds.), *Peer Interaction and Second Language Learning: Pedagogical Potential and Research Agenda* (pp.33-61). Philadelphia, Pennsylvania: John Benjamins Publishing Company.

Duff, P.A. (2012). Identity, agency, and second language acquisition. In S. M. Gass & A. Mackey (Eds.), *The Routledge Handbook of Second Language Acquisition* (pp.410-426). New York: Routledge.

Duff, P. A. (2010). Language socialization. In N. H. Hornberger & S. L. McKay (Eds.), *Sociolinguistics and language education* (pp.427-452). Bristol: Channel View Publications.

Duff, P. A., & Doherty, L. (2018). Chinese second language socialization. In K. Chuanren (Ed.), *The Routledge Handbook of Chinese Second Language Acquisition* (pp.82-99). New York: Routledge.

Duff, P., Anderson, T., Ilnyckyj, R., VanGaya, E., Wang, R. T. X., & Yates, E. (2013). *Learning Chinese: Linguistic, Sociocultural and Narrative Perspectives*. Boston, MA: Walter de Gruyter.

Erbaggio, P., Gopalakrishnan, S., Hobbs, S., & Liu, H. (2016). Enhancing student engagement through online authentic materials. *IALLT Journal of Language Learning Technologies, 42*(2), 27-51. doi: 10.17161/iallt.v42i2.8511

Florio-Ruane, S. (1987). Sociolinguistics for educational researchers. *American Educational Research Journal, 24*(2), 185-197. doi: 10.2307/1162890

García, O. (2009). *Bilingual Education in the 21st Century: A Global Perspective*. Malden, MA: Wiley-Blackwell.

García, O., & Kleifgen, J. A. (2010). *Educating Emergent Bilinguals: Policies, Programs, and Practices for English Language Learners*. New York: Teachers College Press.

García, O., & Sylvan, C. E. (2011). Pedagogies and practices in multilingual classrooms: Singularities in pluralities. *The Modern Language Journal*, *95*(3), 385-400. doi: 10.1111/j.1540-4781.2011.01208.x

García, O., & Wei, L. (2014). *Translanguaging: Language, Bilingualism and Education*. London: Palgrave Macmillan.

Gardner, H. (1983). *Frames of Mind: The Theory of Multiple Intelligences*. New York: Basic Books.

Golonka, E. M., Bowles, A. R., Frank, V. M., Richardson, D. L., & Freynik, S. (2014). Technologies for foreign language learning: A review of technology types and their effectiveness. *Computer Assisted Language Learning, 27*(1), 70-105. doi: 10.1080/09588221.2012.700315

González, N., Moll, L., & Amanti, C. (2005). *Funds of Knowledge: Theorizing Practices in Households, Communities, and Classrooms*. Mahwah, New Jersey: Lawrence Erlbaum Associates.

Gort, M., & Sembiante, S. F. (2015). Navigating hybridized language learning spaces through translanguaging pedagogy: Dual language preschool teachers' languaging practices in support of emergent bilingual children's performance of academic discourse. *International Multilingual Research Journal*, *9*(1), 7-25. doi: 10.1080/19313152.2014.981775

Graff, G. (2001). Hidden intellectualism. *Pedagogy, 1*(1), 21-36. Retrieved from https://muse.jhu.edu/article/26320

Guillot, M. (1996). Resource-based language learning: Pedagogic strategies for Le Monde sur CD-ROM. In E. Broady & M. Kenning (Eds.), *Promoting Learner Autonomy in University Language Teaching* (pp.139-158). London: Association for French Language Studies/CILT.

Hailikari, T., Katajavuori, N., & Lindblom-Ylänne, S. (2008). The relevance of prior knowledge in learning and instructional design. *American Journal of Pharmaceutical Education, 72*(5), 1-8. doi: 10.5688/aj7205113

Hailikari, T., Nevgi, A., & Lindblom-Ylänne, S. (2007). Exploring alternative ways of assessing prior knowledge, its components and their relation to student achievement: A mathematics based case study. *Studies in Educational Evaluation, 33*(3-4), 320-337. doi: 10.1016/j.stueduc.2007.07.007

Halliday, M. A. K. (1985). Systemic background. In J. D. Benson & W. S. Greaves (Eds.), *Systemic Perspectives on Discourse (Vol. 1): Selected Theoretical Papers from the 9th International Systemic Workshop.* Norwood, N. J: Ablex Publishing Corporation.

Han, J., & Yao, J. (2013). A case study of bilingual student-teachers' classroom English: Applying the education-linguistic model. *Australian Journal of Teacher Education, 38*(2), 118-131. doi: 10.14221/ajte.2013v38n2.3

Hanan, J. (2014). *Educational Hip Hop Music in the Classroom: Activating Minds in Creative Ways* (Master thesis). California State University. Retrieved from http://hdl.handle.net/10211.3/123874

Hanks, W. (1991). Foreword. In J. Lave & E. Wenger (Eds.), *Situated Learning: Legitimate Peripheral Participation* (pp.13-24). Cambridge: Cambridge University Press.

Harreveld, B., & Singh, M. (2009). Contextualising learning at the education-training-work interface. *Education+Training, 51*(2), 92–107. doi: 10.1108/00400910910941264

Hedges, H. (2012). Teachers' funds of knowledge: A challenge to evidence-based practice. *Teachers and Teaching, 18*(1), 7-24. doi: 10.1080/13540602.2011.622548

Hedges, H., Cullen, J., & Jordan, B. (2011). Early years curriculum: Funds of knowledge as a conceptual framework for children's interests. *Journal of Curriculum Studies, 43*(2), 185-205. doi: 10.1080/00220272.2010.511275

Herrington, J., Reeves, T. C., & Oliver, R. (2014). Authentic learning environments. In J. M. Spector, M. D. Merrill, J. Elen, & M. J. Bishop (Eds.), *Handbook of Research on Educational Communications and Technology* (4th ed.) (pp.401-412). New York: Springer.

Hirst, E. (2007). Identity construction in complex second language classrooms. *International Journal of Educational Research,46*(3-4), 159-171. doi: 10.1016/j.ijer.2007.09.008

Hohensee, C. (2016). Teachers' awareness of the relationship between prior knowledge and new learning. *Journal for Research in Mathematics Education, 47*(1), 17-27. Retrieved from http://www.jstor.org/stable/10.5951/jresematheduc.47.1.0017

Hymes, D. (1977). *Foundations in Sociolinguistics: An Ethnographic Approach*. London: Tavistock Publications.

Hymes, D. (1980). *Language in Education: Ethnolinguistic Essays*. Washington, D.C.: Center for Applied Linguistics.

Jørgensen, J. N. (2008). Polylingual languaging around and among children and adolescents. *International Journal of Multilingualism*, *5*(3), 161-176. doi: 10.1080/14790710802387562

Karrebæk, M. S., Madsen, L. M., & Møller, J. S. (2015). Everyday Languaging: Collaborative research on the language use of children and youth. In L. M. Madsen, M. S. Karrebæk & J. S. Møller (Eds.), *Everyday Languaging* (pp.1-18). Boston, MA: De Gruyter, Inc.

Kelly, C. (2012). Recognizing the 'social' in literacy as a social practice: Building on the resources of nonmainstream students. *Journal of Adolescent &Adult Literacy, 55*(7), 608-618. doi: 10.1002/JAAL.00072

Kim, H. K., & Lee, S. (2012). Teacher's use of funds of knowledge to promote class participation and engagement in an EFL context. In B. Yoon & H. K. Kim (Eds.), *Teachers' Roles in Second Language Learning: Classroom Applications of Socio-cultural Theory* (pp.121-134). Charlotte, N.C.: Information Age

Publishing.

Kinchin, I. M. (2011). Visualising knowledge structures in biology: Discipline, curriculum and student understanding. *Journal of Biological Education, 45*(4), 183-189. doi: 10.1080/00219266.2011.598178

Kinchin, I. M. (2016). *Visualising Powerful Knowledge to Develop the Expert Student: A Knowledge Structures Perspective on Teaching and Learning at University*. Boston: Sense Publishers.

Koedinger, K. R., Kim, J., Jia, J. Z., McLaughlin, E. A., & Bier, N. L. (2015). Learning is not a spectator sport: Doing is better than watching for learning from a MOOC. In *Proceedings of the Second (2015) ACM Conference on Learning@ Scale* (pp.111-120). New York: ACM.

Lai, K. W., Khaddage, F., & Knezek, G. (2013). Blending student technology experiences in formal and informal learning. *Journal of Computer Assisted Learning, 29*(5), 414-425. doi: 10.1111/jcal.12030

Lankiewicz, H. (2014). From the concept of languaging to L2 pedagogy. In H. Lankiewicz & E. Wąsikiewicz-Firlej (Eds.), *Languaging Experiences: Learning and Teaching Revisited* (pp.1-32). Newcastle upon Tyne, England: Cambridge Scholars Publishing.

Lave, J., & Wenger, E. (1991). *Situated Learning: Legitimate Peripheral Participation*. New York: Cambridge University Press.

Leather, J., & van Dam, J. (2003). Towards an ecology of language acquisition. In J. Leather & J. van Dam (Eds.), *Ecology of Language Acquisition* (pp.1-29). Boston: Kluwer Academic Publishers.

Leeman, A. (2012). Book review: Alastair Pennycook, language as local practice. *Discourse Studies, 14*(1), 135-136. doi: 10.1177/1461445611425718b

Leeman, J., & Serafini, E. J. (2016). Sociolinguistics for heritage language educators and students. In M. Fairclough & S. M. Beaudrie (Eds.), *Innovative Strategies for Heritage Language Teaching: A Practical Guide for the Classroom* (pp.56-79). Washington, D.C.: Georgetown University Press.

Lewis, G., Jones, B., & Baker, C. (2012a). Translanguaging: Origins and development from school to street and beyond. *Educational Research and Evaluation, 18*(7), 641-654. doi: 10.1080/13803611.2012.718488

Lewis, G., Jones, B., & Baker, C. (2012b). Translanguaging: Developing its conceptualisation and contextualisation. *Educational Research and Evaluation*, *18*(7), 655-670. doi: 10.1080/13803611.2012.718490

Li, J. (2017). *Curriculum and Practice for Children's Contextualized Learning*. Berlin: Springer.

Lindquist, J. (2010). What's the trouble with knowing students? Only time will tell. *Pedagogy, 10*(1), 175-182. doi: 10.1215/15314200-2009-030

Mahendra, N., Bayles, K., Tomoeda, C., & Kim, E. (2005). Diversity and learner-centred education. *ASHA Leader, 10*(16), 12-13, 18-19. Retrieved from http://search.proquest.com/docview/218098625?accountid=36155

Marsh, C. (2009). *Key Concepts for Understanding Curriculum* (4th ed.). London: Routledge.

Maton, K. (2014). Building powerful knowledge: The significance of semantic waves. In B. Barrett & E. Rata (Eds.), *Knowledge and the Future of the Curriculum: International Studies in Social Realism* (pp.181-197). New York: Palgrave Macmillan.

Maturana, H. R., & Varela, F. J. (1992). *The Tree of Knowledge: The Biological Roots of Human Understanding*. Boston & London: Shambhala Publications.

McKay, S. (2013). Authenticity in the language teaching curriculum. In C. Chapelle (Ed.), *The Encyclopedia of Applied Linguistics* (pp.299-302). Oxford, UK: Wiley-Blackwell.

McKay, S. L. (2017). Sociolinguistics and language education. In N. V. Deusen-Scholl & S. May (Eds.), *Second and Foreign Language Education* (pp.15-26). Cham: Springer.

McKay, S. L., & Bokhorst-Heng, W. D. (2008). *International English in Its Sociolinguistic Contexts: Towards a Socially Sensitive EIL Pedagogy* (pp.180-199). New York: Routledge.

Mehisto, P. (2012). *Excellence in Bilingual Education: A Guide for School Principals*. Cambridge: Cambridge University Press.

Mignolo, W. D. (1996). Linguistic maps, literary geographies, and cultural landscapes: Languages, languaging, and (trans)nationalism. *Modern Language Quarterly*, *57*(2), 181-196. doi: 10.1215/00267929-57-2-181

Mohammed-baksh, S., & Callison, C. (2015). Hegemonic masculinity in hip-hop music? Difference in brand mention in rap music based on the rapper's gender. *Journal of Promotion Management, 21*(3), 351-370. doi: 10.1080/10496491.2015.1039177

Möllering, M. (2015). Australian language policy and the learning and teaching of Chinese. In R. Moloney & H. Xu (Eds.), *Exploring Innovative Pedagogy in the Teaching and Learning of Chinese as a Foreign Language* (pp.19-37). Berlin: Springer.

Moloney, R. (2013). Providing a bridge to intercultural pedagogy for native speaker teachers of Chinese in Australia. *Language, Culture and Curriculum*, *26*(3), 213-228. doi: 10.1080/07908318.2013.829081

Moloney, R., & Xu, H. (2015a). Taking the initiative to innovate: Pedagogies for Chinese as a foreign language. In R. Moloney & H. Xu (Eds.), *Exploring Innovative Pedagogy in the Teaching and Learning of Chinese as a Foreign Language* (pp.1-17). Berlin: Springer.

Moloney, R., & Xu, H. (2015b). Transitioning beliefs in teachers of Chinese as a foreign language: An Australian case study. *Cogent Education*, *2*(1), 1024960. doi: 10.1080/2331186X.2015.1024960

Moloney, R., & Xu, H. (2018). *Teaching and Learning Chinese in Schools: Case Studies in Quality Language Education*. Berlin: Springer.

Morita, N. (2004). Negotiating participation and identity in second language academic communities. *TESOL Quarterly*, *38*(4), 573-603. doi: 10.2307/3588281

Morton, T. (2013). Critically evaluating materials for CLIL: Practitioners' practices and perspectives. In J. Gray (Ed.), *Critical Perspectives on Language Teaching Materials* (pp.111-136). London: Palgrave Macmillan.

Nguyen, H. B., & Do, N. N. T. (2017). Students' attitudes towards drama-based role play in oral performance. *European Journal of Foreign Language Teaching*, *2*(3), 30-48. doi: 10.5281/zenodo.893585

Nunan, D. (1988). *The Learner-centred Curriculum: A Study in Second Language Teaching*. Cambridge: Cambridge University Press.

Ord, J. (2016). *Youth Work Process, Product and Practice: Creating an Authentic Curriculum in Work with Young People*. London & New York: Routledge.

Orr, S., Yorke, M., & Blair, B. (2014). 'The answer is brought about from within you': A student-centred perspective on pedagogy in art and design. *International Journal of Art & Design Education, 33*(1), 32-45. doi: 10.1111/j.1476-8070.2014.12008.x

Orton, J. (2008). *Chinese Language Education in Australian Schools*. Melbourne, Australia: The University of Melbourne.

Orton, J. (2016). Issues in Chinese language teaching in Australian schools. *Chinese Education & Society, 49*(6), 369-375. doi: 10.1080/10611932.2016.1283929

Ozverir, I., Osam, U. V., & Herrington, J. (2017). Investigating the effects of authentic activities on foreign language learning: A design-based research approach. *Educational Technology & Society, 20*(4), 261-274. Retrieved from http://www.jstor.org/stable/26229222

Pennycook, A. (2010). *Language as a Local Practice*. New York: Routledge.

Qi, J. (2015). *Knowledge Hierarchies in Transnational Education: Staging Dissensus*. New York: Routledge.

Rajuan, M., & Gidoni, Y. (2014). Drawing as a tool to promote emotional health in the EFL classroom. *TESOL Journal, 5*(4), 750-766. doi: 10.1002/tesj.168

Rigby, J., Woulfin, S., & März, V. (2016). Understanding how structure and agency influence education policy implementation and organizational change. *American Journal of Education, 122*(3), 295-302. doi: 10.1086/685849

Rind, I. A. (2016). Conceptualizing students' learning experiences in English as second language in higher education from structure and agency. *Cogent Social Sciences, 2*(1), 1-16. doi: 10.1080/23311886.2016.1191978

Robson, C., & McCartan, K. (2016). *Real World Research: A Resource for Users of Social Research Methods in Applied Settings* (4th ed.). Hoboken: Wiley.

Rowe, A. D., Fitness, J., & Wood, L. N. (2015). University student and lecturer perceptions of positive emotions in learning. *International Journal of Qualitative Studies in Education, 28*(1), 1-20. doi: 10.1080/09518398.2013.847506

Ryu, D. (2013). Play to learn, learn to play: Language learning through gaming culture. *ReCALL, 25*(2), 286-301. doi: 10.1017/S0958344013000050

Sayer, P. (2013). Translanguaging, TexMex, and bilingual pedagogy: Emergent bilinguals learning through the vernacular. *TESOL Quarterly, 47*(1), 63-88. doi:

10.1002/tesq.53

Scarino, A. (2010). Language and languages and the curriculum. In A. Liddicoat & A. Scarino (Eds.), *Languages in Australian education: Problems, Prospects and Future Directions* (pp.157-178). Newcastle upon Tyne: Cambridge Scholars Press.

Scarino, A. (2014). Recognising the diversity of learner achievements in learning Asian languages in school education settings. In N. Murray & A. Scarino (Eds.), *Dynamic Ecologies* (pp.137-150). Dordrecht: Springer.

Schifter, C. C. (2013). Games in learning, design, and motivation. In M. Murphy, S. Redding & J. Twyman (Eds.), *Handbook on innovations in learning* (pp.149-164). Charlotte, NC: Information Age Publishing.

Schuck, S., Kearney, M., & Burden, K. (2017). Exploring mobile learning in the third space. *Technology, Pedagogy and Education, 26*(2), 121-137. doi: 10.1080/1475939X.2016.1230555

Scrimgeour, A. (2014). Dealing with 'Chinese Fever': The challenge of Chinese teaching in the Australian classroom. In N. Murray & A. Scarino (Eds.), *Dynamic Ecologies* (pp.151-167). Dordrecht: Springer.

Scrimgeour, A., Foster, M., & Mao, W. (2013). Dealing with distinctiveness: Development of Chinese in the Australian curriculum: Languages. *Babel*, *48*(2/3), 20-29. Retrieved from https://search.informit.com.au/documentSummary;dn=859138854913290;res=IELHSS

Segal, B. (2014). *Teaching English as a second language through rap music: A curriculum for secondary school students* (Master thesis). The University of San Francisco. Retrieved from https://repository.usfca.edu/cgi/viewcontent.cgi?referer=https://scholar.google.com.au/&httpsredir=1&article=1117&context=thes

Singh, M., & Ballantyne, C. (2014). Making Chinese learnable for beginning second language learners?. In N. Murray & A. Scarino (Eds.), *Dynamic Ecologies* (pp.199-214). Dordrecht: Springer.

Singh, M., & Han, J. (2014). Educating teachers of 'Chinese as a local/global language': Teaching 'Chinese with Australian characteristics.' *Frontiers of Education in China*, *9*(3), 403-428. doi: 10.3868/s110-003-014-0032-x

Singh, M., & Han, J. (2015). Making Chinese learnable: Strategies for the retention of language learners. In F. Dervin (Ed.), *Chinese Educational Migration and Student-teacher Mobilities: Experiencing Otherness* (pp.166-190). London: Palgrave Macmillan UK.

Singh, M., & Nguyễn, T. H. N. (2018). *Localising Chinese: Educating Teachers Through Service-learning*. London: Palgrave Macmillan.

Singh, M., Han, J., & Ballantyne, C. (2014). *Making Chinese Learnable: Research Oriented School Engaged Teacher-researcher Education*. Kingswood, Australia: Western Sydney University Library Collection.

Sleeter, C., & Carmona, J. F. (2016). *Un-standardizing Curriculum: Multicultural Teaching in the Standards-based Classroom*. New York: Teachers College Press.

Smagorinsky, P. (1998). Thinking and speech and protocol analysis. *Mind, Culture, and Activity*, *5*(3), 157-177. doi: 10.1207/s15327884mca0503_2

Smith, D. (2000). Content and pedagogical content knowledge for elementary science teacher educators: Knowing our students. *Journal of Science Teacher Education, 11*(1), 27-46. doi: 10.1023/A:1009471630989

Smith, D., & Lovat, T. (2003). *Curriculum: Action on Reflection*. Tuggerah, N.S.W.: Social Science Press.

Smyth, J. (2010). Critical teaching as the counter-hegemony to neo-liberalism. In S. Macrine, P. McLaren, & D. Hill (Eds.), *Revolutionising Pedagogy: Education for Social Justice within and beyond Global Neo-liberalism* (pp.187-210). New York: Palgrave Macmillan.

Sowell, E. (2005). *Curriculum: An Integrative Introduction* (3rd ed.). Upper Saddle River, N.J.: Pearson/Merrill/Prentice Hall.

Street, B., & Leung, C. (2010). Sociolinguistics, language teaching and new literacy studies. In N. H. Hornberger & S. L. McKay (Eds.), *Sociolinguistics and Language Education* (pp.290-316). Bristol: Multilingual Matters.

Stromquist, N. (2015). Gender structure and women's agency: Toward greater theoretical understanding of education for transformation. *International Journal of Lifelong Education*, *34*(1), 59-75. doi: 10.1080/02601370.2014.991524

Sturak, K., & Naughten, Z. (2010). *The Current State of Chinese, Indonesian, Japanese and Korean Language Education in Australian Schools: Four*

Languages, Four Stories. Melbourne, Australia: Education Services Australia. Retrieved from https://www.education.gov.au/data-and-research-schooling/resources/current-state-chinese-indonesian-japanese-and-korean-language-education-australian-schools

Surmont, J., Struys, E., van Den Noort, M., & van De Craen, P. (2016). The effects of CLIL on mathematical content learning: A longitudinal study. *Studies in Second Language Learning and Teaching, 6*(2), 319-337. doi: 10.14746/ssllt.2016.6.2.7

Swain, M. (2005). The output hypothesis: Theory and research. In E. Hinkel (Ed.), *Handbook of Research in Second Language Teaching and Learning* (pp.471-483). New York: Routledge.

Swain, M. (2006). Languaging, agency and collaboration in advanced second language proficiency. In H. Byrnes (Ed.), *Advanced Language Learning: The Contribution of Halliday and Vygotsky* (pp.95-108). London: Continuum.

Swain, M., & Lapkin, S. (2011). Languaging as agent and constituent of cognitive change in an older adult: An example. *Canadian Journal of Applied Linguistics*, *14*(1), 104-117. Retrieved from https://journals.lib.unb.ca/index.php/CJAL/article/view/19869/21681

Swanborn, P. (2010). *Case Study Research: What, Why and How?*. London: SAGE.

Taylor, T. (2001). Gendering sport: The development of netball in Australia. *Sporting Traditions, 18*(1), 57-74. Retrieved from http://library.la84.org/SportsLibrary/SportingTraditions/2001/st1801/ST1801i.pdf

Tobias, S. (1994). Interest, prior knowledge, and learning. *Review of Educational Research*, *64*(1), 37-54. Retrieved from https://www.jstor.org/stable/pdf/1170745.pdf

Toohey, K. (2000). *Learning English at School: Identity, Social Relations and Classroom Practice*. Clevedon, England: Multilingual Matters.

Tsung, L., & Cruickshank, K. (2011). Teaching and learning Chinese in global contexts: CFL worldwide. In L. Tsung & K. Cruickshank (Eds.), *Emerging Trends and Issues in Teaching and Learning Chinese* (pp.1-10). London: Continuum.

Turnnidge, J., Côté, J., & Hancock, D. J. (2014). Positive youth development from sport to life: Explicit or implicit transfer?. *Quest, 66*(2), 203-217. doi:

10.1080/00336297.2013.867275

van Compernolle, R. A. (2016). Sociolinguistic authenticity and classroom L2 learners: Production, perception and metapragmatics. In R. A. van Compernolle & J. McGregor (Eds.), *Authenticity, Language and Interaction in Second Language Contexts* (pp.61-81). Bristol: Channel View Publications.

van Compernolle, R. A., & McGregor, J. (2016). Introducing authenticity, language and interaction in second language contexts. In R. A. van Compernolle & J. McGregor (Eds.), *Authenticity, Language and Interaction in Second Language Contexts* (pp.1-9). Bristol: Channel View Publications.

van Lier, L. (2004). *The Ecology and Semiotics of Language Learning: A Sociocultural Perspective*. Boston: Kluwer Academic Publishers.

van Lier, L. (2008). The ecology of language learning and sociocultural theory. In N. H. Hornberger (Ed.), *Encyclopedia of Language and Education: Ecology of Language* (pp.53-65). Boston, MA: Springer Science+Business Media LLC.

Verhoeven, L. (1998). Sociolinguistics and education. In F. Coulmas (Ed.), *The Handbook of Sociolinguistics* (pp.389-404). Cambridge, MA: Blackwell Publishers.

Vygotsky, L. S. (1962). *Thought and Language*. Cambridge, MA: MIT Press.

Vygotsky, L. S. (1978). *Mind in Society*. Cambridge, MA: Harvard University Press.

Wang, D., Moloney, R., & Li, Z. (2013). Towards internationalising the curriculum: A case study of Chinese language teacher education programs in China and Australia. *The Australian Journal of Teacher Education*, *38*(9), 116-135. doi: 10.14221/ajte.2013v38n9.8

Wei, L. (2011). Moment analysis and translanguaging space: Discursive construction of identities by multilingual Chinese youth in Britain. *Journal of Pragmatics*, *43*(5), 1222-1235. doi: 10.1016/j.pragma.2010.07.035

Wei, L. (2014). Who's teaching whom? Co-learning in multilingual classrooms. In S. May (Ed.), *The Multilingual Turn: Implications for SLA, TESOL and Bilingual Education* (pp.167-190). New York: Routledge.

Wells, G. (1986). *The Meaning Makers: Children Learning Language and Using Language to Learn*. Portsmouth, N.H.: Heinemann.

Wells, G. (1999). *Dialogic Inquiry: Towards a Sociocultural Practice and Theory of*

Education. New York: Cambridge University Press.

Wenger, E. (1998). *Communities of Practice: Learning, Meaning, and Identity*. New York: Cambridge University Press.

Wenger, E., McDermott, R. A., & Snyder, W. (2002). *Cultivating Communities of Practice: A Guide to Managing Knowledge*. Boston, MA: Harvard Business School Press.

Whitley, M. A., Farrell, K., Maisonet, C., & Hoffer, A. (2017). Reflections on service-learning: Student experiences in a sport-based youth development course. *Journal of Physical Education, Recreation & Dance, 88*(7), 23-29. doi: 10.1080/07303084.2017.1340202

Winch, C. (2013). Curriculum design and epistemic ascent. *Journal of Philosophy of Education*, *47*(1), 128-146. doi: 10.1111/1467-9752.12006

Winston, J. (2014). Second and additional language learning through drama. In J. Winston & M. Stinson (Eds.), *Drama Education and Second Language Learning* (pp.1-5). New York: Routledge.

Yiakoumetti, A. (2012). Bidialectism and aboriginal language education: Sociolinguistic considerations pertinent to Australia's aboriginal communities. In E. Esch & M. Solly (Eds.), *The Sociolinguistics of Language Education in International Contexts* (pp.169-194). New York: Peter Lang.

Yin, R. K. (2018). *Case Study Research and Applications: Design and Methods* (6th ed.). Los Angeles: SAGE.

Yuan, Y., Tangen, D., Mills, K. A., & Lidstone, J. (2015). Learning English pragmatics in China: An investigation into Chinese EFL learners' perceptions of pragmatics. *The Electronic Journal for English as a Second Language*, *19*(1), 1-16. Retrieved from https://eprints.qut.edu.au/84645/

Zhang, G. X., & Li, L. M. (2010). Chinese language teaching in the UK: Present and future. *The Language Learning Journal*, *38*(1), 87-97. doi: 10.1080/09571731003620689

Zhao, H., & Huang, J. (2010). China's policy of Chinese as a foreign language and the use of overseas Confucius Institutes. *Education Research Policy and Practice, 9*, 127-142. doi: 10.1007/s10671-009-9078-1

Zhu, P. (2010). A historical perspective on teaching Chinese as a second language. In

J. Chen, C. Wang & J. Cai (Eds.), *Teaching and Learning Chinese* (pp.33-72). Charlotte, N.C.: Information Age Publishing.

Zipin, L. (2013). Engaging middle years learners by making their communities curricular: A funds of knowledge approach. *Curriculum Perspectives, 33*(3), 1-12. Retrieved from Western Sydney University Library Collection.

Glossary

绘声绘色(huìshēnghuìsè) means that something is described in a very vivid way and lifelike style through presenting its sound and appearance.

就地取材(jiùdìqǔcái) is defined as obtaining materials from the local area to make full use of the potential potency of local resources.

朗朗上口(lǎnglǎngshàngkǒu) refers to a genre with certain rhythms, such as verse or poetry, which is easy to read aloud and remember the content.

量体裁衣(liàngtǐcáiyī) literally refers to tailoring according to a person's actual figure or height. Metaphorically, it means that carrying something out should be based on actual circumstances.

人尽其才(rénjìnqícái) means that everyone can do their best to complete some tasks or deal with some difficulties through fully utilising their own advantages and abilities.

融会贯通(rónghuìguàntōng) refers to achieving the mastery of new knowledge through combining it with the existing knowledge comprehensively.

身体力行(shēntǐlìxíng) refers to earnestly practising and experiencing what has been learnt.

物尽其用(wùjìnqíyòng) refers to making the best use of everything available, such as materials or resources in order to get them to serve their proper purpose.

喜闻乐见(xǐwénlèjiàn) means what one really loves to hear and see, which is extremely popular among people.

学以致用(xuéyǐzhìyòng) means putting what has been learned into practice during the process of learning some abstract knowledge.

因地制宜(yīndìzhìyí) literally means taking suitable measures or making reasonable decisions to deal with something that should be based on the local specific conditions, especially as they occurred and applied in the field of agriculture.

主人翁意识(zhǔrénwēng yìshí) means a sense of ownership and belonging.

图书在版编目（CIP）数据

超语视角下澳大利亚小学中文课程的本土化构建 = Localising Chinese Language Curriculum Construction for Australian Primary School Students: Translanguaging Lens : 英文 / 赵昆鹏著 .-- 杭州 : 浙江大学出版社，2023.12
ISBN 978-7-308-24448-0

Ⅰ. ①超… Ⅱ. ①赵… Ⅲ. ①汉语－对外汉语教学－本土化－教学研究－澳大利亚－英文 Ⅳ. ①H195.3

中国国家版本馆CIP数据核字(2023)第234961号

超语视角下澳大利亚小学中文课程的本土化构建

Localising Chinese Language Curriculum Construction for Australian Primary School Students : Translanguaging Lens

赵昆鹏　著

策划编辑　陆雅娟
责任编辑　陆雅娟
责任校对　杨诗怡
封面设计　项梦怡
出版发行　浙江大学出版社
（杭州市天目山路148号　邮政编码　310007）
（网址：http://www.zjupress.com）
排　　版　杭州林智广告有限公司
印　　刷　广东虎彩云印刷有限公司绍兴分公司
开　　本　710mm×1000mm　1/16
印　　张　12.5
字　　数　282千
版 印 次　2023年12月第1版　2023年12月第1次印刷
书　　号　ISBN 978-7-308-24448-0
定　　价　50.00元

浙江大学出版社市场运营中心联系方式：0571-88925591；http://zjdxcbs.tmall.com